Winner of the Fifth Annual
EX OPHIDIA PRESS PRIZE FOR POETRY
2020

To Speak in Salt

Other Books by Becky Thompson

Making Mirrors: Righting/Writing by and for Refugees. Co-editor, Jehan Bseiso.

Teaching with Tenderness: Toward an Embodied Practice.

Survivors on the Yoga Mat: Stories for Those Healing from Trauma.

Zero Is the Whole I Fall into at Night.

When the Center Is on Fire: Passionate Social Theory for Our Times. Co-author, Diane Harriford.

Fingernails across the Chalkboard: Poetry and Prose on HIV/AIDS from the Black Diaspora. Co-editors, Randall Horton and M. L. Hunter.

A Promise and a Way of Life: White Antiracist Activism.

Mothering without a Compass: White Mother's Love, Black Son's Courage.

Names We Call Home: Autobiography on Racial Identity. Co-editor, Sangeeta Tyagi.

A Hunger So Wide and So Deep: A Multiracial View of Women's Eating Problems.

Beyond a Dream Deferred: Multicultural Education and the Politics of Excellence. Co-editor, Sangeeta Tyagi.

To Speak in
Salt

Poems by
Becky Thompson

Ex Ophidia Press
2022

James T. Jones. Publisher.
Richard-Gabriel Rummonds, Publisher Emeritus and editor.
Sharon Cumberland, Director of the Poetry Prize Contests.
Gregory C. Richter, copy editor.
Richard-Gabriel Rummonds, design and typography.
Reece Johnson, layout editor.
Brad Hutchinson, graphics consultant.
John D. Wagner, public relations and marketing.

Photos on pages vi and 97 copyright © 2022 by Becky Thompson.
Publication Acknowledgements are listed on page 110.
Map and waves by Marcia Breece.

Published by
Ex Ophidia Press,
17037 10th Avenue NE
Shoreline, WA 98155.
exophidiapress.org

Thompson, Becky, 1959-
To speak in salt / Becky Thompson

Paperback ISBN 978-1-7373851-1-0

for
Arezu Kabuli
Katherine Larson
Diane Genevieve Harriford

All respect to people forced to leave their homelands,
these poems are for you.

And who will join this standing up
and the ones who stood without sweet company
will sing and sing . . .
even under the sea
— June Jordan
Directed by Desire

Table of Contents

Part Three

Part Four

Preface

In her beautiful book *Afterland*, the poet Mai Der Vang writes, "Spirit, we are in this with each other the way the night geese / in migration need the stars."[1] This is how I feel about the worries of the world, that we are in this together to solve them, whether it be the climate catastrophe or the pandemic or forced migration. The language for a new century requires that we see how these worries are connected and that we all know that "love calls us to the things of this world."[2]

When by happenstance I found myself meeting rafts of people fleeing war in Syria, Afghanistan, and other countries to Lesvos, Greece, in 2015, my first yearning was to welcome people arriving on the shores and provide supplies as they made their way across the island. In the first few months, the media had not yet arrived, a reality that led me to write articles for international news outlets. By early summer, the media brought their cameras, which alerted the world to the enormity of the forced migration, even though most reports were *about* people in transit, not *by* them.

When I returned to Boston in 2016, I felt bereft, mute even, desperately wanting people to know about the enormity of the exodus and the courage of those in transit, but weary of the quickly fixed and contained imagery of "the refugee." During this time, a friend sent me Jehan Bseiso's online poem "No Search, No Rescue," dedicated "to the families and lovers at the bottom of the sea, trying to reach Europe."[3] I had watched dinghies on the horizon disappear, held grandmothers and children who could not stop shaking, and walked with Syrian and Iranian poets up the mountain pass, their poems a talisman as people climbed. Jehan, a seventh-generation Palestinian poet working in Lebanon, agreed to edit a volume of poetry by and for refugees. From a café in Beirut, we put out a call for submissions and received stunning poems from people across the globe, though none from current asylum seekers. Their missing voices led me to offer poetry workshops on mainland Greece and in Lesvos which enabled us to publish *Making Mirrors: Righting/Writing by and for Refugees* with poems by people still on the move alongside those in more secure places.[4]

As a white poet based in the United States, I felt my first responsibility was not to write about people in transit but to use resources I had to get their poems published.[5] Once *Making Mirrors* was published, I turned to my own writing. Like many people, I was having great difficulty conceptualizing the enormity of forced migration in this century. In 1903, W.E.B. Du Bois wrote that the "problem of the twentieth century is the problem of the color-line."[6] I began to see that the problem of the twenty-first century is the problem of the borderline and that those two problems are linked. I turned to poetry rather than prose, realizing that certain topics require a deeper register. Complex sentences and footnotes flattened what I had witnessed: mothers feeding infants out of paper cups because their baby bottles had sunk, Afghan activists making a radio station out of egg cartons and tin cans. I came to see those generically referred to as "refugees" as artists, aunts, professors, bricklayers, and activists who risked their lives on tiny rubber dinghies to save their lives.

Retrospectively I am struck by how many times I circled back to the arrival of rafts — a location of great presence and absence. In *The Art of Time in Memoir* Sven Birkerts explains that writing is "the restoration through words of what has otherwise vanished from the world."[7] My experience is that the slip of sea between Turkey and Greece holds a multitude of consciousness. While trauma can bind people to each other in inexplicable ways, it is also an eraser, requiring us to find words for what is missing, including parts of ourselves. During a living nightmare, time can feel interminable and rapid, seared into memory, yet too intense to remember.

As artists we search for time. There are some events whose horror, whose immensity, puts them in the category of lost time — the time between the policeman aiming at Philando Castile's chest and pulling the trigger, the time from rafts leaving Turkey's shore to making it to the beach in Lesvos (or not). Certain life struggles demand that we find words. Some time carries more weight, a yearning, an insistence, a simultaneous pulling back and moving forward. This willingness to grapple with lost time may become the energy woven into Faith Ringgold's quilts, the cutout images in Kara Walker's art, the resonant words in Yusef Komunyakaa's poem "Facing It."[8] These elegant works of art don't bring back the dead. Their accomplishment is more humble; we are caught inside certain extraordinary moments, trying to shrink them to something fathomable, or find ways to live with them. In Lesvos, I needed to tack moments down, to create a witness.

* * *

Going back and forth to Greece, I have continued to ask questions about subject position and creativity, particularly of people who are both insiders and outsiders to what they write about. I think of Carolyn Forché's astounding witnessing in El Salvador during the U.S.-sponsored war. There was a forty-year stretch between when "What you have heard is true" appears as the first line in her 1978 poem, "The Colonel," and when it became the title of her 2019 memoir.[9] Forché's U.S. citizenship required that she hold her government accountable for the atrocities she saw.

Tarfia Faizullah, a Bangladeshi-American poet, also reckons with insider/outsider complexity in her delicate book *Seam*.[10] As she renders visible the genocidal rape of 200,000 women in East Pakistan in 1971, Faizullah insists on placing herself within the narrative, not positioning herself as an observer "studying" rape victims. She sidelines the where, when, and how of rape, a tedious linear retelling that can feed voyeurism, in favor of light touch, respectful references. Instead of gruesome details, the poet highlights the repetition of senses, of color, shape, and sound, a quintessential linguistic pattern for many trauma survivors.

As someone who grew up in Iran but now lives in the U.S., the celebrated poet Sholeh Wolpé also dances between cultural contexts in her work. While many poems in her book *Rooftops of Tehran* are sweeping and global, those in *Keeping Time with Blue Hyacinths* are more interior.[11] The metronome of this later book is the back and forth between pain and beauty, with pauses in the middle for martinis, tango, and taking to the bed for escape. Still, the voice of a world conscience is present, as she continues to write of the invisible, twisted, multiple lives of exile. Paul Celan also straddles the border between the living and the dead — he whose family died in the Holocaust while he lived.[12] His poetry is haunted by this inexplicable sparing. There are so many eyes in his poems, watching in the silence. Repetition becomes a safety net, connective tissue in narratives that are, by definition, missing pieces. Traumatic memory is not like "regular" memory. It is like a long piece of film that has been spliced, with many pieces left lying on the floor. It is up to the survivor, the poet, the lover, to pick up some of the pieces, unworried about putting it all back together, accepting brokenness as its own beautiful frame.

While these and other poets model ways to reckon with subject position, discovering how to do that myself was often messy, confusing, fraught. In "A Sketch of the Past" Virginia Woolf asserts that writers tend to say, "'This is what happened': but they do not say what the person was like to whom it happened. And the events mean very little unless we know to whom they happened."[13] How might a poet expose her changing perspectives, emotions, and complicity, without taking over the narrative, without re-centering an external gaze?

One approach I fell upon as an insider/outsider was through persona poems from the point of view of a raft, a prison wall, the sky. Conjuring up these non-sentient beings required imagination, which, at first, I resisted. As an activist, I have learned vital history from poets who stick close to the "facts": June Jordan going to Nicaragua, Rafael Campo working with people with AIDS, Naomi Shihab Nye writing on Palestine.[14] I wanted my poems to be historically accurate. Who am I to embellish, to move beyond facts?

But over time, I have seen that if I don't use my imagination, I risk flattening descriptions of people and places. My meetings with many asylum seekers were so intense, quick, urgent. There wasn't time for me to even ask, "Where are you from? What languages do you speak? Where is your grandmother?" I came to see that even when I didn't have the "facts" the emotive imagery stayed with me — the curve of a young woman's back as she held her newlywed's hand; the vivacious transwoman who said, "Yes, even on the raft I wore my silk scarf." Without imagination, people and places remain one-dimensional. Still, I found myself asking: Whose story is this? Who gets to tell what, ethically?

While there are no simple answers, I remember a young woman who told me how healing it was when she saw a video made by a Greek advocate that included footage of her family getting off the raft in Eftalou. She spoke of it as a moment of integration, as if the big details of the journey could be fastened down a bit. Might poems be like that for people, a way to secure a feeling, not leave blank spaces, moments floating with no name?

* * *

As a life-long reader of poetry, I have often wondered about a poet's shifts in consciousness as they write. I wonder, for example, if there was a specific moment of awareness when Ilya Kaminsky decided to set *Deaf Republic* in an unspecified place?[15] How was it for Anna Akhmatova, those decades when *Requiem* was only held in the memories of ten friends, not on the page?[16] When did Paul Celan feel most alive, which poems, which country? The recent rise in hybrid writing may help mend some of the Aristotelian splits that still police literary borders. I am drawn to poetry that "collapses the distance between writer and reader," an intimacy that makes space for vulnerability and beauty.[17]

My biggest shift in consciousness has come through understanding how "poems can slip into places that people and politics cannot."[18] I knew that was true for world class poetry, by Neruda, Du Fu, Hikmet, Jordan, and Lorde, since their poems have flown around the globe, have been woven into presidents' speeches, city walls, political banners. But what about poets who don't have such a big reach? I had my doubts about the power of words to undo cruelty. But while teaching poetry workshops, I watched participants delight each other with their poems. In places where we didn't have blackboards, we hung up butcher paper on walls so people could write their poems. In storerooms where there was no available wall space, we recited poems to each other. Kurdish, Sunni, Christian, Palestinian, Sudanese elders, and youth wrote collective poems in multiple languages on paper that woke up classroom spaces. One accomplished Syrian painter I met used lipstick for paint to cover the walls of the cubicle where she was staying with her six children. She and her close friend arrived at a workshop with a chapbook of poems they had written while crossing borders.

Another change in consciousness involves my growing respect for formal forms. When I started writing poetry, Sonia Sanchez advised that I only write haiku for the first year, her antidote for my sociological writing. Since then, I've learned how villanelles and pantoums provide structure for difficult subjects. Compression creates internal combustion as words become nuggets of energy inside the line. Toni Morrison writes, "The work must bear witness and identify danger as well as possible havens from danger."[19] Some poems need to gain momentum and then settle, since the topics themselves — people drowning, people in limbo in frozen tents — present their own crashing. The restraint of carefully counted syllables cuts away nonessentials so that only deep meaning remains.

Alice Walker has written, "A writer's heart, a poet's heart, an artist's heart, a musician's heart, is always breaking. It is through that broken window that we see the world: more mysterious, beloved, insane and precious for the sparkling and jagged edges of the smaller enclosure we have escaped."[20] I included this quote in poetry packets in Farsi, Dari, Arabic, and French, made possible by translators with whom I had the privilege to work. Teaching with, and being taught by, translators is a riveting experience. Intimate, like a dance, exhausting, part hilarious, part pitiful, as I continue to learn so many cultural cues. Another quote I included is from John Edgar Wideman: "The sign of silence presides over my work. Characters who can't speak, won't speak, choose never to speak until this world changes. My impulse to give voice to the dead, the unborn, to outlaws and outcasts whose voices have been stolen or muted by violence . . . . Silence is proof that the decision to listen or not is ours. Proof that we are called to pay attention."[21] This call to attention made its way into "We Have Taken the One in the Sky as Our Witness" in honor of Fadwa Souleiman, a beloved actor and activist in Syria who died young of cancer. Souleiman's death speaks to a plethora of losses people are facing: loss of community, years of missed school, disconnection from first languages, family members strewn about. The map of where people are staying looks like the dangling threads of slave trade routes. Since Moria burned down and many NGO's left, government plans for new arrivals closely approximate prisons — closed containers fit for no breathing beings. Lesvos, one of the most welcoming islands on earth, is now split geographically and politically.[22] People have faced Golden Dawn, dwindling pensions, plummeting tourism, and young people having to leave small villages for work. Greece is the little guy in comparison to the other EU countries making the economic decisions. Meanwhile, U.S.-enforced travel bans led me to ponder if, in a few thousand years, the humans will arrive. If the planet is still willing to host them.

And then there is the land itself. Lesvos is a crossroads for birds from all over the world. As small as the island is, it still contains four different terrains — high desert, seashore, petrified forests, and plains. You can see a long line of Turkey's coast from Lesvos. Most people there have relatives in Turkey. In the long view of time, Turkey and Lesvos are actually one piece of earth. When rescue boats began stopping rafts from coming to shore, they eliminated a way for people to land in beauty, to stand on the beach, to see where they came from, to adjust their hats and scarves before taking the next steps. The beauty of Lesvos holds people; it can't help it. That holding is a counterbalance to human cruelty. Maybe not enough. But still. And continuing.

In this collection I ask how language might create a space to bear/bare witness. Poems carry contradiction and balance — atrocity with humanity, the forces of love with the forces of loss. Disorienting darkness and intoxicating beauty. In forced migration, children are often the most hurt and the most imaginative; love lives in crevices, in glances, and with newcomers willing to hold up protest signs even as they risk deportation. Resistance is never-ending for people living as "guests of the wind."[23]

Notes to the Preface

1. Mai der Vang, *Afterland* (Graywolf, 2017), 20.

2. Richard Wilbur, "Love Calls Us to the Things of This World," *Collected Poems 1943-2004* (Harcourt, 2004), 233-234.

3. Jehan Bseiso, "No Search, No Rescue," *Electronic Intifada*, April 24, 2015, http://bit.ly/2uZe83N.

4. Jehan Bseiso and Becky Thompson, editors. *Making Mirrors: Righting/Writing by and for Refugees* (Interlink Books, 2019).

5. This is a lesson I learned from multiracial feminism: solidarity is not a given for white women; it is earned. Lorraine Bethel, "What Chou Mean We, White Girl? Or, The Cullud Lesbian Feminist Declaration of Independence (Dedicated to the Proposition that All Women are Not Equal, i.e., Identical/ly Oppressed)," *Conditions: Five: The Black Women's Issue*, 1979, 86-92.

6. W.E.B. Du Bois, *The Souls of Black Folk* (Penguin Classics, 1989), 13.

7. Sven Birkerts, *The Art of Time in Memoir: Then, Again* (Graywolf Press, 2008), 20.

8. Yusef Komunyakaa, *Neon Vernacular: New and Selected Poems* (Wesleyan University Press, 1993), 159.

9. Her memoir can be read as a companion to *The Country Between Us*, a lesson for poets, an Ars Poetica about what makes poetry possible. Carolyn Forché, *What You Have Heard is True: A Memoir of Witness and Resistance* (Penguin, 2019); Carolyn Forché, *The Country Between Us* (Harper & Row, 1981).

10. Tarfia Faizullah, *Seam* (Crab Orchard Review, 2014).

11. Sholeh Wolpé, *Keeping Time with Blue Hyacinths* (University of Arkansas Press, 2013); Sholeh Wolpé, *Rooftops of Tehran* (Red Hen, 2008).

12. Paul Celan, *Selected Poems and Prose of Paul Celan*. Translated by John Felstiner (Norton, 2011).

13. Sven Birkerts, *The Art of Time in Memoir: Then, Again* (Graywolf Press, 2008), 26.

14. Rafael Campo, *What the Body Told* (Duke University Press, 1996); June Jordan, *Living Room* (Thunder's Mouth Press, 1985); Naomi Shihab Nye, *The Tiny Journalist* (BOA Editions, 2019).

15. Ilya Kaminsky, *Deaf Republic* (Graywolf, 2019).

16. Anna Akhmatova, "Requiem," *The Complete Poems of Anna Akhmatova*, edited by Roberta Reeder. Translated by Judith Hemschemeyer (Zephyr Press, 1997), 384 - 404.

17. Kim Addonizio and Dorianne Laux, *The Poet's Companion: A Guide to the Pleasures of Writing Poetry* (Norton, 1997), 118.

18. Katherine Larson, personal correspondence.

19. Toni Morrison, *The Source of Self-Regard: Selected Essays, Speeches and Meditations* (Knopf, 2019), 267.

20. Alice Walker, "Edwidge Danticat, the Quiet Stream," Facebook. January 23, 2010. 1:49 p.m., http://alicewalkersgarden.com/2010/01/Edwidge-danticat-the-quiet-stream. April 2020.

21. John Edgar Wideman, "In Praise of Silence," *The Writing Life: Writers on How They Think and Work*, edited by Marie Arana (Public Affairs, 2003), 117.

22. In this way, the collection traces forced migration in phases. The first, when people were walking to Europe (2015-March 2016); the second, after the borders closed (March 2016-2017); the third, long term limbo (2017-2019); and the current imprisonment of recent arrivals (2020-present).

23. Mahmoud Darwish, *If I Were Another.* Translated by Fady Joudah (Farrar Straus Giroux, 2009), 173.

Personal Acknowledgements

In his poem "A Trace," Rumi writes, "you that give new life to this planet, / you that transcend logic, come. I am / only an arrow. Fill your bow with me / and let fly." Katherine Larson, you have been my bow, your learned presence, a lifetime.

Also, Debra Marquart, your playfulness and confidence in me.

Chen Chen, your intuitive guidance.

The writing of Anna Akhmatova, Carolyn Forché, Sonia Sanchez, Ilya Kaminsky, Joy Harjo, Natalie Diaz, Daniel Borzutzky, Ocean Vuong, June Jordan, Tarfia Faizullah, Audre Lorde, Jalaluddin Rumi, and Sholeh Wolpé.

Friends and family: Sally Abood, Ginny Onysko, Zeina Azzam, Sharif Elmusa, Randall Horton (always), John Cort, Caroline Reger, Dwayne Betts, Howie Goldstein, Saloni Kumar, Sumeya Ali, Victoria Story, and Fred Marchant.

All respect to Jalal Joinda, Philippa and Eric Kempson, Nadia Ghulam, Sayed Naweed Balkhi, and Merna Ann Hecht. Love to Maryam Janikhushk and your family, for trusting me with your daughter, Arezu Kabuli, as she studies all living things.

Thank you to Mary and Ignatios Kazantzoglou for your Sun House, to Zoe Holman for *Where the Water Ends*, to Angela Farmer, who called me to Lesvos, and to Diane Harriford, who brought me there.

Thank you to the Mosaik Support Centre and the Hope Project (Lesvos), the Khora Centre (Athens), and the Elpida Home (Thessaloniki) for allowing me to teach "Love Calls Us to the Things of This World" poetry classes from 2016 until Covid slowed us down.

My appreciation to Robin Talbot for her resounding encouragement, the Stonecoast Social Justice Scholarship, and the Simmons University Research Fund.

Prelude

In 2015-2016 over one million people from Syria, Afghanistan, Iraq, Somalia, Iran, Palestine, Pakistan, and other countries fled violence in their homelands to Turkey where they took dinghies across the Aegean Sea to the Greek Islands. Among these islands, Lesvos became the center of the passage into Europe. After arriving, families walked across the island as they made their way to the Greek mainland and on to northern European countries. What was identified as the biggest refugee crisis since WWII was also the biggest intergenerational, multilingual peace march in modern history. While the number of people reaching Greece has declined since the EU closed borders in 2016, the crossings continue. With nods to Sappho, Minoan pots, and silhouettes crossing the burning sun, this collection focuses upon the lives of people in transit as it circles around my years meeting rafts, walking with people, and teaching poetry in refugee centers.

Lead Witnesses

Sand: willing to hold a raft's imprint until the next high tide.

Keys: from houses in Syria kept on a ring under diapers in a satchel.

Satchel: carried or thrown overboard if a raft is sinking.

Poetry: climbs mountain passes, is tucked into the Quran, sung in verse.

Lesvos: made from a volcano, Lepetymnos. Quiet now.

Moria: the biggest refugee "camp" in Europe that burned to the ground in October, 2020.

Fire: leaps across tents, devours passports, pacifiers, date meat, olive trees, and shade.

Part One

Words made of island sand
Words that have known the pottery of the sea
Words rolling in

> — Josué Guébo
> *Think of Lampedusa*

We Say, *Salt*

Salt in fine lines around your eyes   keep walking
Salt in the shaker   where tourists stare
Salt for flavor   salt caged in yellow plastic   salt to make tabouleh
In Arabic salt is milh   we say salt is earth's silk
For the desert's pleasure   we say salt in the blood
We say   salt will dust your eyes with sorrow   come here I will kiss you   here
Sprinkle salt for tomatoes   salt for when your lover leaves you in salt
When the bomb leaves a salt trail in the street   we scatter with our children
Salt tracks on the desert   travel at night   with salt in our shoes
The sea loans salt to rocks   we are salt   rafts our own salt nation.

The Sea Shares Salt with the Breeze

1

The poppies stand at attention, like stop signs
among twisted life jackets, cut-up water bottles,

men's pants strewn across surprised hills.
It's true, the road is drenched in light.

Cassandra rolls up a tattered raft, stacks
baby life jackets (the size of juice cartons),

the orange still inflated. A family inches
toward Molyvos, tells us they silenced

the motor to muffle their landing. Rain
threatens the blue expanse. The sea chants.

2

They tell me, we chanted, our raft
took in water like an upside down

umbrella. We stayed still, zipped up
our breath until we reached sand, our

lips, dried roses. Xenos in Greek means
foreigner and guest. Police caution

walk west, no shelter here.
Our eyes paint forward.

3

Their shoes walk, I sleep
awake. My mind

confuses helicopter blades
for fishing boats, a buzzing

refrigerator for a motorcycle.
When a light zigzags across

black glass, I wave a lantern
in big sweeps above my head

to guide the silhouettes to shore.
We share chai and plum toast.

Families walk, babies
in arms at the back.

4

Nations: canopy each raft,
                a human chain
to carry dazed relatives
                from the boat to shore,
who gather under an
                eastern strawberry tree
its thin skin shed in
                long strips. We drink water
and load my bike again
                one child on the front
another behind, handlebars
                carry diapers and apricots.
In Kalloni they spread
                a blanket over a bare floor
lay their infants down like tired
                dandelions drowned by sun.

5

Tired sun: cancel rough-sea days. Our eyes count whitecaps.
A man in a torn wetsuit drags a dinghy to shore, euros all wet.
Scavengers eat bananas. Rusty pickups haul engines to sell in Izmir.
A father lifts his newborn to Allah. Everybody cheers.
Girls in Kmart shirts with smartphones ask about Sylvester Stallone.
At night I pass food through open shutters, toss water bottles.

6

We snuck families into her tinted-windowed van, the Greek chef and I,
dodged police barricades, sped
                          families to safety across the island.

After that, we shopped for sweet kale and marzipan
at the gourmet grocery.
                    She had stopped smoking by then

except after the dinner rush or before the dinner rush. Sometimes
in the middle. She was beautiful
                              to the end with her brilliant bald head.

She taught me the five drivers of this migration:
sex slavery + organs + water + arms + drugs.
                                SOWAD,

an acronym we made up. Rhymes with firing squad, Assad,
façade, retinal rod, roughshod, cephalopod,
                                    war god, not outlawed.

Cephalopod, from the mollusk class, characterized by the ability
to squirt ink. Known to fishermen as ink fish.
                                    Another name for poets?

SOWAD: the people in vans kidnapped in Bulgaria missing now.
One December, I watched a Serbian vet jerry-rig
                              a car radio

to intercept patrol boat messages. We liberated sneakers
from a storehouse
                  when wind chill reigned.

The lesson. Find the key. Use the key. Replace the key. Repeat.

7

What about the mother who tucked her infant
under the prow
        of a docked boat, the only shade where

the baby could sleep? It's true babies can sleep
with their eyes open
        when you rock them in a van,

heading to Mantamados. If you're walking from
Afghanistan to Turkey,
        waterproof Band-Aids are gold —

like rosaries made of green olive pits by inmates
at the Damascus Central Prison.
        Pure ingenuity.

Like the Lesvos Dirty Girls in trucks, who hoist piles
of wet clothes to the laundromat,
        bring them back clean

for the next boats. Smelling like jasmine. The girls wear
suspenders and purple rain boots.
        I've always liked a girl

in uniform. In Mantamados, the legend of St. Taxiarchis
honors the embossed image of the saint
        made from mud

and blood of murdered monks. They say the saint changes
shape depending on how he
        feels about the believer.

People bring him iron shoes so he can walk at night.
They are found worn out
        the next morning.

8

On days when I want to reach a raft shuttered by cliffs, to find people
who might be too injured or too stunned to talk or out of water or seasick
or unsure which direction to walk, I take a shortcut through the hot
springs gate Yorgos left unlocked without saying a word, when the hot springs
were closed, when Greeks were forbidden to help, a gate that opens to a cove
beyond the naked beach, a rocky route to the sea quicker than any
motorcycle as I jump between stones, an art learned in a rushing
river in northern Arizona with my barefoot sister, tomboys
leaping tall rock buildings in a single bound, legs stretched
like the scent of hyacinth in spring far from Mythimna Road.

9

On Mythimna Road
            an elderly farmer pulls his pickup
to the side, lets eight
            of us pile into the bed
of his truck between
            boxes of nectarines and hay.
Jude's velvet hat hugs
            her eight-year-old head
as her mother stretches
            her own leg out, cut to the bone by
a smuggler's machete.
            They stick a baseball cap
on my head to hide me
            from vigilantes skulking around.
Laurel trees blur by
            and the sea gifts blue
to the farmer who
            saved us from a blazing
walk up a hairpin
            mountain. Jude's father
casts safety with
            his wide-open arms.

10

Past hairpin mountain, two sisters and their kid brother run to the playground
by the Kalimera Resort Hotel, giggle on the slide and candy-striped swings
until a sad-sack manager appears, shoos them away, their parents saying
Salaam Alaikum, sorry, aietidhar. My little sister and I played pirates
one Christmas and took apart our Swing Set with shiny wrenches and
screwdrivers. I wish for our toolbox so we can double back.

11

When talking   is our only toolbox   on a double moon night
a musician explains to me:

> rubble   pinned spirits   to the ground   when the drones
> came running   toward   our house   each day
> a meteor shower   the pink white walls   collapsed
> around us   we packed   my flute   and phones
> scooped water   with hands like bowls   as waves
> competed   for the sky's attention   we traced
> the route   ancestors   traversed when
> Turkey   was still   Asia Minor.

12

Minors: channel ancestors. The bowl of the earth
is turning upside down, ti kaneis and khoda hafez

barely a start; the teens teach me Persian
phrases, khosh amadid and dooset daram

my mouth marbles, they laugh. A tourist
bus snorts up a starless hill, numbers walk.

13

Numbers dizzy the stars. One million walk
across the border, two million hover to cross, three

million in transit, four million stuck, five
million pray, six million killed in the Holocaust.

Germany, the refugees' goal, this paradox.
Elie Wiesel wondered if God died

in Auschwitz? I want to ask: the boy who
fills a baseball cap with cool water; the man

in Kara Tepe as he observes salat, sewage a street
beside him; the mother, deaf from a barrel bomb,

collapsed on the beach, then hoisted herself
up, dressing her daughter in a pink Madeline hat;

the family who outsmarted the smugglers,
found their own raft, snuck under the radar;

the professor who ran alongside my car; placed
his only blue stone ring on my finger —

Aftermath: Counting in Greek

The war came to shore shaped like a watermelon slice
They wrapped their cell phones in plastic, tore up their passports
The helicopter picked up people except when wind stirred the sky
We couldn't count the rafts that sank
On a day when a second raft vanished, the sea refused more rain, clouds stained black
The point is to add shape that doesn't end in zero
What does a museum look like for splintered boats and lockets caught in fishing lines?
Workers painted walls orange in Kara Tepe, teens stared at make-believe calendars
Sticks became guns, bombs in the sky flowered children's drawings
A white-pillared house stands idle in Eftalou and lights dizzy the coast of Izmir
On the beach where they sliced raft bellies with fishing knives, yellow beach chairs
wait for tourists.

Dido's Lament

In Aleppo, we'd play with words, evanescence
and effervescence, our conversations electric,
mornings at TcheTche Café for half a baguette
and fig marmalade, cardamom coffee, extra
cream, the neighbor's drab shawl, her eyes on us, our eyes.

And before we met, I'd take a fast train
to Istanbul, laugh all night with a Danish journalist
who couldn't taste lemon drops nor stay
silent. We watched a marine, his wide
holster and yesterday smeared across his skin.

Summers before, I temped as a translator
in an auditorium designed for sound,
my words exact. On Fridays
I'd take the city bus to the Souq, wander
through the Bedouin fabrics, taste the curried soup.

These trips, evanescence. You, in my life
effervescence, the guts to go when we did, with
my clarinet and your doctor's bag, my music trapped
in vinyl. I convinced you, after the café scattered
stained glass across the floor.

When you jumped from the raft to lighten the load
to swim, or so you thought, who knows, the driver
refused to go back. I begged for you in three tongues.
Later, they searched the Gulf of Adramiti.

I crouched into a trance as reporters circled for a story.
The Greek coast guard shouted like I didn't speak English.
Or French. Or read Russian. My hands didn't tremble. Yet.

Minutes after they found you clutching air, the reporter
pressed, aren't you relieved? My mouth a silent wail.
No. I am furious. He didn't ask me before he jumped.
The raft still married water. A seahorse in my belly.

A Litany Travels

The translator says: *Let's turn to* A Litany for Survival.
We'll say it first in Dari. Then English. All together. Ready?

Did I mention that I'm over my head?

Or perhaps my head continues to fly about but my spine has folded in.

When did this accordion behavior begin?

Was it when we had chairs for fifteen and twenty-five came, not
counting the children?

Or was it when I passed around an attendance sheet that came back with six
signatures? Fear buried their pens.

Was it after we read a haiku and a father said, *how can we write pretty poems,
our lives are not pretty*, as his three-year-old daughter drew on her arm
with a purple marker?

Or was it when I couldn't outline the basic shape of Afghanistan on the board?
Someone came up, drew his country and all the ones that touch it.

Was it when shutters we opened so the small room could breathe kept banging,
each time pulling people from their chairs?

An older man rose and gently closed the shutters.

Or was it when a teenager clutched her friend, sandwiched between men
like fish, said she liked the poem about memories and backpacks, wished it was
in Somali. I said, *me too*.

Or was it when a father explained his family receives 300 euros each month. If
they're granted asylum, that will end after six months.

Or was it when I was sure two teens who stared into their phones were there for the free bus tickets until they recited brilliant landays in Dari and English. They wrote them with Google Translate.

What about the seven-year-old who answered all my questions in English before the adults, their eyes stuck on the table.

       The table floating with cherry pits left by the four-year-olds.

There is no childcare at this refugee center.

Parents hold their children close, won't let them go farther than their side vision.

       Their eyes reach in all directions.

The Afghan filmmaker declares, *I'd rather not hear the word refugee. Ever again.*

He asks, *What would happen if every time you hear the word refugee you* ~~whisper~~ / *shout the word* people?

What about the woman who, after I blah blah about writing to tell the truth says, *with all due respect, no one can speak honestly as long as we are here.*

Layla Asks, *Why Are We Here If We Didn't Do Anything Wrong?*

When it's cold I can see my breath, tiny
crystals inside little clouds. We carry
branches from the forest to our tent.
Papa says the wood is dead. So it's okay
to burn. Except for olive trunks. They're
still alive. Like sleeping cats. More like
resting than dead. Mama says that without
olive trees I wouldn't be here. Great-
grandmother to daughter. Great-grandfather
to son. That's the line. Olive farmers.
Soap makers. Cooks in fancy restaurants.
Olive oil for fried zucchini flowers and
crispy potatoes. We don't burn olive trees.
It would be like burning ourselves.

Yesterday the family next door —
we say next door even though it's a tent —
packed up to move to Kara Tepe, a funny
word I had to practice. It costs a lot to move.
Again. Kara Tepe is closer to town. People
live in containers, not tents. Mama says
a container is a box where no mosquitoes
are allowed. It has a door we can close.
And a flat floor. Still no room for my sister's
tricycle. Papa says the sky will be blue
wherever we go. At night mama whispers
when they think I'm asleep. Says she's
a bad daughter for leaving my grandma
behind. That we might get sent back.
Even though our house is gone. The
school's blown up. Says, we're hungry
here. White rice is not enough.

There's a woman here who carries me
on her shoulders. Even though I'm big.
She teaches poetry, sings us songs. *We
who believe in freedom cannot rest.*
It's from these singers she calls Sweet
Honey in the Rock. I didn't know rocks
have honey. That teacher is from America
where the bombs that fell on our house
come from. Now I wonder, who is who?

Mama says sometimes I ask too many
questions. Papa says we're strong
enough for anything. We have
olive trees in our blood. Mama says,
use your imagination. Like the drawings
we make in class at the Mosaik Centre.
As if painting smoke can carry a message.
The art teacher wishes the bombs we draw
could turn to hearts. I tell her I can say
good morning in six languages. French
from the girl two tents away. Dari and Arabic
from Sami who stays in Kara Tepe. Farsi
I knew. English, of course. And Greek
for the streets, at Lidl's grocery store. I draw
bombs that look like bombs. I save hearts
for real bodies. Sometimes the whole body
can be a heart. Lots of red on the page.
Papa says we're lucky. Mama says
don't lie to the children.

Zouhourat, An Invitation

In the months when you could walk from
the highway right into Kara Tepe people
would escort you, arms circling,

> *yes, happy to see you, and I remember your purple*
> *leather backpack, and yes, my arm is better, the one*
> *we wrapped in plastic from the dry cleaners to stop*
> *the bleeding and this is my daughter who was shaking*
> *after the crossing, and here is my grandmother who*
> *you walked with into town and yes, I can take you*
> *to the family who arrived last week, the elder*
> *is a teacher, about fifteen all together, yes, they are*
> *Syrian from Idlib and be careful not to step in*
> *the dirty water, and we can't eat the food here*
> *since it made my family sick, all twelve of us,*
> *and yes, we arrived after the second day of walking*
> *so long, too hot. But we're all here. We're dry after*
> *everything got soaked that day the men cut the raft,*
> *took the engine before we even got out. Not sure how*
> *long we will wait. We gave our names several*
> *times. Careful where you're walking and down*
> *this lane, to the right, is their tent . . .*

The elder reaches his arms out, *Salaam Alaikum,* his eyes
a welcome party. Says,

> *duck your head. So glad you found us.*
> *Remember my wife and mother from the beach?*
> *Here's my brother and his children. It's tight but*
> *we're together. Sit on this cushion. Thank you*

for bringing the heart medicine. And SIM cards
to call our family. God be with you. Will you
join us for tea? Zouhourat made from hibiscus.
How does it taste? Yes, perfect sweetness.

Part Two

Very little grows on jagged rock. Be ground.
Be crumbled so wildflowers will come up where you are.

— Jalal ad-Dīn Muhammad Rumī
The Soul of Rumi

Ahmad Talks to His 13-Year-Old Brother

Remember you are Superman, with a hurt-proof cape. Don't forget your aunt nick-
named you Balloon — he who will float above danger.   Learn to draw a map of
Syria in ink on paper cups.   Don't look at the sea if it makes you sad. Look
at the sea and remember you made it.   Be the song you sang on the raft.
Don't run from ghosts.   Use your backpack as a pillow, a seat, a table.
Carry your prayer rug inside.   It's okay to let the rug double as a bed.
Eat meals with the young Palestinians.   They've been through this
longer than you have.   Keep ironing your shirts even though you
have to stand in line. Know your people are proud. Remember
why they sent you first.   Don't trade your toothpaste for
cigarettes. Well, maybe sometimes. Don't sell your
kidney to anyone. Ever. Remember your uncle
before the sniper. Be tall. Know you come
from a people of maps and stars. Learn
how to be a barber. Wherever you go
men will need their hair cut.
Don't drink bleach.
Don't drink bleach.

Jamil Says, *We Wait in Line*

Afghan School, Mitilini

Close to swerving into down and low. We
watch the coast guard swear in Greek as they dare to strike.
It's painful to lose months, moldy cots stacked straight.
Hard if you've played percussion in Jalalabad and taught physics. We
outran the drones and kissed our mothers' hands. Many can sing
so now we trade hip-hop beats — Awesome Qasim meets Soul Travelers. Sin
was dreamed up by the military and electrified borders. We
know it's easy to gain days with Allah if you're dead. Thin
chance. We know Taliban trucks were made in the USA, gin
and heroin fast-tracks for military who rape by day. We
are *clouds looking for a way out, gotta play no matter the sway of forces.* We jazz
a new plan, pool our money, buy tents for a school, open in June,
two years later children still come. And elders — Kurds and Somalis. We
teach music and mathematics, world politics wrapped in rap. We will not die
soon.

Ghazal: Asylum for the Youngest Brother

Their bodies thrown from Afghanistan, they escape by sea,
for three years Greece offers shaky shelter, who will see?

In Moria they barter for cigarettes, stand in queues, with
grandmothers who said they were forced to trust the sea.

They build a radio station with egg cartons and sweat, send
Dari and Arabic through airwaves to enlighten the sea.

They spread prayer rugs under a tamarisk tree,
its parasol safer than tents stacked by a wild sea.

Their videos expose Moria's hunger and neglect.
Officials punish their brother. What they don't want to see.

They wait for months, time like a basket empty of bread;
deportation separates them like teacups fallen in the sea.

How to sleep without night sweats after bombing in Kabul?
Their parents now in exile by the Indian Sea.

At a mushaira they gather lilies for the dead. Can you hear
their mother sing their names by the sea?

His girlfriend whispers in German, honeysuckle
on her skin, her auburn hair awakens him. He sees.

Whose names will you remember? Shaped like the arc of the sea.
Joinda, their sovereign family, robust across the sea.

Immigration

I can't offer you
evidence since my backpack
sank to the bottom.

Coping

This is not funny.
I am laughing. You are laugh-
ing. Pass the pita.

Solidarity, (For)ever

1

In Eftalou, surreal life jackets strewn like a painting, Syrian students
show me a video of a poetry slam

in Damascus. One man from Qamishli asks about Tupac Shakur.
That night I call my mother, her voice

a low viola, who tells me about ancient Arabic etched into pottery.
She studied in Qamishli, whispers, *they're*

gassing children, bombing the mosques. I'm too embarrassed
to ask, where's Syria on a map?

It's two countries west of Afghanistan, on rafts with young
guys from Pakistan. Find a map.

We scribble map routes from Eftalou to Mitilini, on paper
napkins. They're walking across the island.

Young yogis raise money on Facebook so we can buy baby
bottles, tuna, maxi pads, baguettes. But don't buy

dates. If people have anything, it's that delectable fruit mothers
pull from their bags after the last disaster.

Each family a chosen date.

2

It's an honor to be offered a date, to witness the birth of new life
when jubilation circles the beach

but a father reaches for a diaper from his bag and pulls out
a key for a house that is obliterated.

The door gone, the key remains, a diaper for his child but —
he shows me photos.

I retrace my mother's steps, her only true love, a Lebanese man
who taught Dostoyevsky.

He called her habibti, a word that breathes now on this island.
When someone asks you to choose

one spelling for habibti — habeebi, habibi, habibni —
what can you do? Keep them all.

3

How come I keep   coming back   something about safety
something about home   in second grade   I paste a slave ship
on blood red paper   I'm on   that ship   a little girl tied down
the one who   flees her body   knows it's not home   for years
in dreams   the Gestapo smash   my front door   strap me
down   in a forsaken place   I feel myself   in Anne Frank
Alan Kurdi   so what to do with   this intimacy   this over-identifying
funnel money   from friends   to buy baby bottles   live for dates.

4

My friend Gabriel tells me, there's been twelve thousand
volunteers in Lesvos since 2015,
                              only fifty in Yemen.

Why? Idyllic views, the finest olive oil, romantic coves,
quick flights from Athens.
                              Racism that refuses to sink.

There's still raw sewage in Moria. Gabriel said head honchos
make five thousand dollars each month,
                              Greek workers, a fraction.

He says, ship the bosses back to Brussels. Give the money
to the locals and newcomers. Meanwhile
                              the Greek system moves

like a tortoise in the sun, years in limbo. In 2015 everyone
fleeing to Greece walked north.
                              Now Greece is their only hope.

Today Arabic and French bounce down cobblestone streets.
An old woman stands on tiptoes
                              squinting into the ATM

as she searches for her pension. A Pakistani teen tilts
with his tall body
                    to shade the screen from the sun.

5

There are (at least) three ways to connect with people across borders.
Feminist as tourist. Terrible.
Feminist as explorer. Not good.
Feminist in solidarity. Not easy.

6

An English tourist tells a shopkeeper she wants to welcome people
to Lesvos. He asks,
                    why not greet them in your home country?

An American volunteer picks up a family whose baby is sick
then cranks the Christian music
                              so loud the mother can't hear

the doctor's voice on the phone. In Athens I pass out a packet
of poems just before class,
                         discover the Farsi script runs

left to right. Before I apologize a woman points to the poem
with Aleppo in the title, says,
                         Let's start here. I'm from Aleppo.

The class admires the poem even though the poet
a seventh generation Palestinian
                              has never lived in Aleppo.

7

On days turned upside down with injuries, a certain elder yogini
her hair like Medusa
                        and a spine she can roll up

and down a Lesvos volcano — she who feeds forty cats, swims
in the Aegean winter —
                        shows up with her jeep

for a shivering man in a wheelchair, three children and their mother
who can't stop shaking.
                        One morning two sea-soggy girls

run up hills searching for a fishing boat to rescue a raft. They tell
me they're seventeen years old.
                        When I see them later, they say, *nineteen*.

Haiku Questions

Is a poem really
a poem if it's written on
someone else's back?

Can there be any
refugee poetry that's
not by refugees?

Who owns words if they
are in the sea? Can dolls talk
once they wash ashore?

Call Me Cosmopolitan

poetry workshop for youth, Thessaloniki

I wear black boots with silver buckles, teach myself on the Internet.
Before the raft I got a tattoo. My mom's name so she will know.
They call rubber dinghies floating coffins. They don't charge less in a storm.
I have one kidney. My brother is here with me. He is worth the price.
I speak Somali. Andam speaks Pashto. Adh speaks Farsi. So, we all laugh.
After Dadaab, me. After Libya, me. After the sea, we.
I like this poem about wild geese and flying. My father writes at night.
I practice English, perform for volunteers. Learn to swear on the Web.
My girlfriend sends me a selfie on Fridays. We break our fast on WhatsApp.
We play shoot-'em-up videos on our cots, wait for dinner: cold cuts.
Sometimes I'm so hungry I eat baby food from the storage room.
I call home with phone cards bought from turning tricks. Steal the mint mouthwash.
How come they hate us in the U.S.? I have a Beyoncé tee shirt.
The first seventeen years of my life don't count. I am starting over.

We Have Taken the One
in the Sky as Our Witness

In your right hand hold the colour of the tribes,
in the left, a pencil that erases state borders.

With the colour of dawn you can cross over,
a merciful God turns a mirror on borders.

For if you have crossed, so have we all,
skin is an organ that refuses all borders.

We plant petunias in fallen white helmets,
the scent travels past bullets, slips around borders.

Alawites in Aleppo, my family strewn about,
I know now the moon cancels night borders.

If you are worried *grasp a skein of sunlight*,
so torture won't seep into your body's borders.

They call me Fadwa Souleiman, my poems: no borders.
My body from Paris to the sky, an elegant boarder.

Hold onto Time

Beyond the off-white metal door
down the hall past the electric chair
and the dank room where men use
the flying carpet to splay women,

their spines like split rivers, stands
a wall ten feet high, in the cell where
women trace Arabic calligraphy
with their fingertips. A makeshift

blackboard or date book for those
without pencils. Yara Badr called
it an improvised calendar
counting the days inside, scribbles

that run like EKG lines. Perhaps
Yara's father engraved her name
in delicate script on a prison wall
when she was a child. She etched

her husband's name now. When women
get thrown inside, the wall keeps watch
as inmates make toys from matches, sew
coin bags from torn trousers. Before

Yara's husband was taken, his body,
not his spirit, he wrote the line, *I feel*
sorry for us all, meaning those who man
the flying carpet and those strapped

below, each caught in a terrible storm.
Call the wall Robben or Attica
or Abu Ghraib. Related by mortar
and blood. Made of steel feathers.

Carola Rackete Takes the Microphone

My life a change from Silversea cruises
to arrest on a gangplank, my spree against death.

Who knew that I would sink their command?
Powered past an Italian patrol boat, a marquis for the dead.

Since when did rescue become a swear word?
On the fourteenth day I said, *so help me, no dead.*

When an Italian minister claimed my rescue meant war
I said, his words are a quay for the dead.

The photos now shutter my non-normative hair.
Where are stories of migrants whose lovers are dead?

If they impound one ship, we'll raise money for more.
Luventa and *Alan Kurdi* from a fleet that's not dead.

May maritime law stand up against death.
They call me Carola Rackete, I refuse to play dead.

Winnipeg

Conceived in stink, plastic melting like burning flesh,
waterproof seams stitched with needles, doubled back
to reinforce — my birth, my death — ignoble, my body

a vessel for leaving. Between the factory and dump,
I waited. When a smuggler ordered five families
to rush the storm, they refused, afraid the waves

would devour. The smuggler pointed at Samin,
pigtails hiding behind her uncle's legs. *Go now*,
or *there will be no later*. He snatched at a woman's

dress. At the shore parents catapult children over
my slippery edges. Hungry rocks taunt. A man knots
his wheelchair to my handles. My sides expand,

puffed air and plastic, thin as skin. If I were human,
I would ask my ancestors to help. What's the lineage
of a raft — recycled umbrella, lining of a tent,

a billowing sail? *Keep your body as quiet as sleeping
fish*, I whisper to the children. The parents strain
their eyes, scan the distant shore for waving arms.

Silver pellets flood my belly, from below,
fish eyes watch. Between weighted sea and sky,
I gather the threads that circle my body

and I winnipeg us, hoist to safety. To shore.
Families tumble out, a scavenger takes his knife
to my guts. I am limp on the sand, tossed

on a pile of empty water bottles, consigned to Life
Jacket Graveyard. You might not have heard me
say goodbye. But I did. Look up. I may be a balloon,

someday brimming with helium, high for a celebration.

Squatters' Rights

LGBT Gala

Squatting in an abandoned building in Exarchia Square
Qamar and Samir up the ante of who can shimmy faster
Unlock their hips to the jerry-rigged sound system
As the gay chef from Syria orchestrates a four-course dinner
That will stretch to feed fifty. An Afghan couple wanders in,
Their toddler dancing with a transgender woman with
Eyes that tell us, my sisters and I risked the raft,
Ravages of bombs now behind us, a hole in the boat the
Size of my fist, we filled with singing until we were
Rescued. *Paris Is Burning* travels to Athens on a dinghy,
Inclusion the mantra folded into tabouleh, parsley translates from Arabic to Urdu,
Gracious becomes a verb everyone is granted, as the bass from the sound system
Hijacks old fear. *Temporary* becomes an excuse for let's party, community
Travels with tattoos and silk scarves. The toddler sleeps in the crook of an arm as
Silence equals death transforms into eyes from this storm.

Part Three

You run outside, our spirits go with you.

— Naomi Shihab Nye
The Tiny Journalist

The Accompanied Minor Wonders

At first it was a whim, a whisper
before curfew on a bus.
Let the old man see it, then touch.
Ten euros and a phone card for a month.

Before curfew on a bus
in Victoria Square behind a dumpster,
thirty euros, and a phone card for a month.
His hand a chisel, my face a manhole cover.

In Victoria Square behind a dumpster
my parents message me on WhatsApp.
His hand a chisel, my face a manhole cover.
I wear a jacket of secrets, my voice sunken flowers.

My parents message me on WhatsApp.
A young man beckons, his gaze draws me to him.
Asks, why my jacket of secrets, my voice sunken flowers?
His fingers surprise, I'm alive to his touch.

The young man beckons, his gaze draws me to him,
asks, what's worth a dead space inside?
His fingers surprise, I'm alive to his touch.
Let me not be a coward.

What's worth a dead space inside, I wonder.
Let him see me and touch.
Let me not be a coward —
At first only a whim, then a whisper.

Loving in Doorways

Mosaik Centre, Mitilini

We read the lines in the poem about *bread*
in our children's mouths so their dreams
will not reflect the death of ours.

I ask, what dreams will you keep alive?
A teenager offers, I couldn't go to school
my mother's dream already dead.
The room sputters sadness.

I suggest let's practice words for feel:
Good, fine, okay, the standard refrain until
I interrupt, say, no copycat. We do *copy*,
act out *cat*, an expression like *burst at*
the seams, like *loving in doorways*. I stand
in the narrow doorway, lean in and out, ask,
how is it to love here *coming and going*
in the hours between dawns?

A teen gestures to his heart, then
to the east, then to his stomach, we
figure it out, heart sick, almost — Oh!
Homesick. We practice the word out loud:
Homesick. Homesick. Homesick.

Then more words spill: *devastated,*
depressed, worried, oppressed. Indigestion,
a word from the last class. We laugh.

Another youth, red henna hair, gold chain,
diamond post in his left ear says, *my name*
is Abdul Aziz Ahmadi and I feel normal.
On this day, this moment of grace, this gay
teenager with his friends feels normal in

this cacophonous place, my undercover
queer self officially retraced.

My name is Mohammed Zakir and I
feel mountain. The baby on his shoulders
laughs as English expands, we say
mountain-us, mountain-us reigns
above *good* and *fine* and *okay*.

Report from Sona

I count to eighty / in Greek, the boys say Guinea / is a hen, not home.
Mommy says my bike / waits by my ngoni in / our house by the sea.
Dad tucks the Quran / inside plastic at night so / our tent will stay safe.
They shoo the people / we shoo the cats, but who do / the cats shoo? The rats.
I whisper, Dulce / you were brave in the water / Dulce doesn't talk.
When I go outside / I hide Dulce inside my / pillow, she hates dirt.
Do you know who makes / insulin, is that Allah's / job mommy needs it.
When Daddy swings me / round and round, the kids line up / they call him Swing Set.
The boys tease me that / lullabies are for babies / I sing in Susu.
My panties are tight / mommy cuts the elastic / so my legs are loose.
How do clouds hang in / the sky? Do they want to come / down or stay up there?
They call me Sona / aka Diabaté / the lady who sings.

Jeopardy

My mother and father live in _____ now. Where is?
They stabbed my cousin _____ times. What is?
We buried our passports in the sand in _____. Where is?
Sofia is the capital of _____. What is?
We flew to _____, we paid the smuggler in _____ and _____. How much is?
The beach where we landed is _____. What is the name of?
The girl on Facebook they killed is _____. Who is?
My oldest brother is alive and famous. Not a question.
My parents are in _____, my son is in _____, I will live in _____. Where is?

Cartography in Lesvos

Near the oleander bush a family
    hides before their climb up Petra Mountain

after their raft sucked salt water, turned their bellies
    upside down. Over the crest children

dizzy the merry-go-round, dance
    in resort sprinklers until the owner

mumbles generations, hands us aurora
    apricots and vanilla ice cream.

At the praying mantis rock, a science teacher
    with elegant muscles gives me his salmon

shirt, his friends order selfies. Phones telegraph
    safety, lovers sit close, their feet in Europe.

They say memories fade, mine multiply.

Now police intercept rafts, mechanic rescues,
    whisk people away, arrest taxi drivers

who offer free rides. No time
    to stand together in a breeze

What does it mean to miss the intimacy of disaster?

At Life Jacket Graveyard next
    to the dump, a German couple

scooters up the hill, takes photos
    while eating nine-grain toast. French

academics talk postmodern flight.
    A Barcelona film crew picks through

jackets to curate their best shot.
    Crows memorize the wind

as two garbage trucks trudge up with
    old fish and more jackets.

I wave to the sheep herder
    as I skid down the hill.

       Save the people, bury the dead, photograph the remnants. Repeat.

At a computer store the Greek
    man won't copy my poems since

he sees Arabic on the page.
    I sit in his smoke,

ask about his family, eye his automatic
    weapon perched next to the door,

a recent fixture along with
    for sale signs on lonely hotels.

       Down the highway is a new bar next to Moria. Of course.

Greek workers guard people in tents,
    barbed wire doubles as a fence,

a clothesline for diapers, a baby carriage
    seconds as a grocery cart, shade

for an infant, a step up from when parents
    carried babies and toddlers walked.

At the ~~refugee~~ center men grow rings
    around their arms at a makeshift gym,

drink Turkish coffee, dance holding
    hands. Women stretch out like

elaborate stories, by windows
    that mirror the sea.

        The sidewalk sparkles an atlas in transit.

The streets of Mitilini look like Beirut
    Greeks here who ran from Turkey

Turks who kicked out Afghans
    Afghans who wish they were Syrian

Syrians joined by Congolese —
    teachers, holy seers, and men selling hats.

Sappho's Legacy

A family walks until they reach a monastery. Kids play
        in a fountain, adults sleep until sky turns to

afternoon. By the same marble statue, Golden Dawn visits
        two weeks later, leaving graffiti in mixed-up Arabic. The spray-

paint men follow newcomers across the island. My friend
        shows up for the Moria work crew to catch wind

of who's in Golden Dawn. A few beers later Greek workers
        name the five men from Athens with spray paint.

My friend and his buddies find them by their pickups and
        say, it's time to pack your things.

Here's the ferry schedule. We would be happy to escort you
        without the cops, here at the crossroads

built on Sappho's lyrics, carried in a sheepskin satchel,
        her words for soft and mighty days.

In Moria We Have Cats

Crazy cats, high cats, new cats, old cats
Come to play and learn to fight cats
Rich cats in shiny white vans rented for cats.

There are stealing kinds of cats
Take the tent out from under your pillow cats
Cats who sell crack.

Careful you might become a cat
Make money as a cat
Get cat food, sleep with a cat.

Don't feed the cats, whatever you do
No photos, no trinkets
No stories for cats.

Celan Travels

After two friends lift Ra'Ed up a cliff
reporters stage photos of agony
then leave him stranded without a lift

by unshorn sheep and a blue farmhouse. We
sit as he details how his brace split, points
to his spine where a bullet sang tragedy.

The night stuns needlepoint stars, cold anoints
silence until a van arrives, takes us
to the police. I scour the town for joints

to fix plastic, duct tape superfluous.
A Greek jeweler holds the brace in his hands,
melts silver in gaps, wraps a wire truss.

At daybreak I sneak past the camp's command
find Ra'Ed under a juniper tree.
He marvels at the jeweler's winged bands,

straps on the brace so he can stand. We
take a selfie before a final goodbye
as I teach I teach my heart to sleep.

Teaching Poetry at Khora

Praise this stand-alone building in Athens for its ingenuity

Praise the class when their collective poem majors and minors in despair

Praise another class when their poem conjures sunny carousels

Praise the man from Côte d'Ivoire who says,
> *I have no time to write about my past*

Praise him again when he says,
> *I have no time to write about the future*

Praise the Eritrean woman who glances at the door when I ask if she speaks Farsi

Praise the mural on the classroom wall that got carried away with color

Praise the teenager who wrote,
> *they shot us as if we were deer*

Praise the soldier from Syria who asked,
> *can we write about anything, even if it's scary?*

Praise the teenager who wrote haiku about his eight cousins,
> *my mother became / their mother, not enough / to go around*

Praise the artist who wrote in Arabic,
> *the sea did not save my memories or my paintings*

Praise the Syrian woman who wrote,
> *the white postbox stood / alone / the bomb took everything else*

Praise the man from Sierra Leone who leans in,
> *this one in the story who lost his whole family, was me*

Praise the twelve-year-old who whispers,
>*I carry my soul in my hands*

Praise the mother who wrote,
>*I sleep with the sea, I do not sleep.*

A Tailor Explains

the way to begin is to thread the needle. Find
thick ones to poke through heavy canvas. Yes,
we become ghosts that bullets can't find.

Our children catch lightning bugs at night
their feet quick stitches that don't reverse;
the way to begin is to thread the needle. Find

a pattern to embroider Hafiz's poems. We hide
under wild oak trees, other families join us.
We become ghosts that bullets can't find.

Our bodies layers of lace, I stitch a design
for the divine inside my baby's vest.
The way to begin is to thread the needle. Find

the day when the sea was a soft hemline.
Sew a map to safety in our minds.
We become ghosts that bullets can't find.

This night, we sleep outside the tent, side
with wind that unravels the heat, pray
to thread another needle, find
other ghosts bullets could not find.

Ceasefire

Beyond the paned window
        the city glimmered bombs,
our girl a thin wind when
        she walked to school,
the next apartment reduced
        to tilted door frames.

when we were young

nights when tabby cats stopped screaming,
        we unbuttoned, remember
summer by Latakia Harbor, your eyes
        an etude, how even now
your neck stretches, lips
        part, I part you with
permission, your dazzled moon;

nightmare, in love

months now, we talk until we can't,
        about the queues, crushed weight.
This cubicle, could it be?
        Our daughter asks for nothing,
her scared kitten eyes,
        picks at the plastic food
says it tastes like Martians.

to feel safe again, love

and yet, under the borrowed blanket
        I cup your ankles, trace
circles around your belly, wait
        for your slight rise,
darkness arouses us still.

How Shall We Divide This Bounty?

for Nadia Ghulam, Hope Project, Mitilini

In a storeroom stacked with black and blue suitcases,
caved-in boxes, futons that float in dust, eight women
and their children arrive. The storyteller whispers
Bood nabood, once upon a time, the children's faces turn
to her like dinnerplate dahlias. In a land with many animals,

they meet, as animals do. The lion says to the tiger, the fox
and the wolf, go out and get us dinner. The animals
obey the lion, file out, then return: the tiger with a hefty cow,
the fox with a puffy chicken, the wolf with a delectable sheep.

The lion roars to the wolf, *wolf, how shall we divide*
this bounty? The wolf replies, *since the tiger brought*
the cow, he shall eat the cow. The fox, the chicken. And I,
the wolf decides, *shall eat . . .*
                    his words stop mid-sentence
                              the lion has cut off his head.

The lion roars to the fox, *fox, how shall we divide this bounty?*
The fox says, *you shall eat the cow for dinner, the sheep*
for breakfast, and the chicken for a snack. The lion smacks
his lips, says, *and how did you know the answer, dear fox?*
                    When you killed the wolf.

One child claps. Another reaches for her mother's breast,
slips inside her scarf. The storyteller asks,
now what if the animals are countries?
                    Who's the lion? The tiger? The wolf?

The room animates, all agree, *America is the lion.*
Turkey, the fox. Greece would be the sheep.
A young woman interrupts, *No, Greece*

would be the chicken, eaten by Germany
who is the tiger. So is Russia. A woman with
eyes painted black says, *Afghanistan is not*

a fox, she is not a chicken. We are deer,
meat so sweet that everybody wants to eat. The Russians
and Americans are carnivores. Another woman
                    pipes in, *what if we are the lions?*

You walked from Iran with your children. You survived;
your father stolen by a sniper. We're all lions.
Mid-sentence, three women announce they'll be back
as they hurry toward the nervous food line, dinner

scarce, the children sprint in front. The storyteller waits
to resume her tale, her arms embroidered by a bomb, she
who dressed as a boy under the Taliban, traveled

by night to buy jam and bread. Soon, mothers will return,
potatoes rolling off paper plates. New children will arrive.
The storyteller, touched by a southern star, begins again.

In Molyvos an Innkeeper Explains

in Greek we have a parable about a neighbor's goat.
Two neighbors live in a rocky village. One has a goat,
the other is goatless, claims the goat will cavort with
his sheep, make his neighbor rich. The mayor offers to buy
the goatless man a goat, but the man screams, I don't
want a goat, only that my neighbor has no goat.

You see, Germany decides how many goats, which
goats, maybe no goats. In Greek there's a word,
vitrina, the curtain that hides the real show. NGOs
are hungry for goats and travel to shear them. The
Chinese want a railroad to transport goats. Europe
and the U.S. want angry goats to stay outside their

fences. Syria offers rocky terrain for extended goat
killing. Iran pays young Pakistanis to fight in Syria,
kills defectors and defenseless goats. The U.S. sells
weapons to the bidder with the most goats. ISIS laughs
as we watch which mosque, which clock explodes next.

When rescuers wiggle babies and elders from rubble
their relatives carry them to Greece. If they take a
night raft it's cheaper, called the student special.
Once engines reach Lesvos they are re-sold to Turkey,
twenty-first-century recycling to pay for goats.

Women who fled from Izmir to Mitilini in the 1920s
took goat milk baths each day. Greeks called the
Turkish women prostitutes. Now, in Moria, there's
no place for women to wash their hair. On Mondays
they sign up for a bathtub at Bashira House so they
can wash in bubbles and roses, sometimes goat milk.

Calculus

In a makeshift camp, two signs blow in the wind,
Syrians and *All Other Nationalities*. Parents hold babies
and follow signs. My mother dragged my sister and me
from her father's Mormon house after he voted for Wallace,

drew her own line in Arizona sand. This is a story about
who belongs and doesn't. In Athens, Tracie grabs my hand,
marigold scarf flung around her slender neck, says it's safer
for trans women on the streets than in camps.

My friend Luiz and his family dimmed their headlights three times
to cross from Mexico. Each time they were boxed. The fourth
time they walked under a generous moon. A Syrian family
climbed into a raft five times to reach Greece. Thirteen people,

one thousand euros per head, including children. Multiply by five.
Life jackets extra. This spring they bulldozed Lesvos beaches to bring
new sand for tourists. Two million people wait in Turkey. Erdogan
shuffles the money deck. Europe takes a post-WWII bow after they

accept seven percent who fled their homelands. Ninety-three percent
fled to Turkey, Lebanon, and Jordan. In a video, a researcher flips
a monkey on her back, muscles limp, her eyes a closed chapel.
I climb a hill where we watched for rafts with our naked gaze.

Ten kilometers lie between Turkey and Lesvos. Seventeen
hundred between Libya and Italy. The Mediterranean plays
a rigged referee. An expression in Dari, don't search for angels
on the ground, look up. This calculus makes my eyes burn.

Now four Mormon students on a mission eye the sea with
a telescope. Their bishop told them to spread Smith's gospel
to everyone but Muslims. The Latter Day meets the College
of the Americas meets the U.S. border patrol meets Assad's gas.

A Father Asks

for Sayed Naweed Balkhi and his family

We survived the night in the sole of a ship,
from Lesvos to Athens, our eyes infrared.
Vigilantes circled the families at Hotel Daedalip.
We hid our boys under a feather bed.

From Lesvos to Athens, our eyes infrared,
we sent you photos with a blurred skyline.
We hid our boys under a feather bed,
snuck away after the moon fell to Orion.

We sent you photos with a red skyline,
five of us walking with our shoes distressed.
We snuck away after the moon fell to Orion.
I typed in Serbia on my phone's GPS.

Five of us walking with our shoes distressed,
we slipped through a border, absent a barbed fence.
We typed in Serbia on my phone's GPS.
So far from Rumi, but no room for regret.

We slipped through a border, absent a barbed fence,
escaped the Taliban and Golden Dawn.
So far from Rumi, but no room for regret.
I ask: how to be a father with a Sufi song?

We escaped the Taliban and Golden Dawn.
Vigilantes circled the families at Hotel Daedalip.
I ask: how to be a father with a Sufi song?
We survived the night in the sole of a ship.

A Coast Guard Officer Asks

Months after walking with families
to the harbor where Yannis Papadakis

handwrites the names of each newcomer
sometimes patient with Arabic and Farsi,

sometimes wound up, no words
between us, my actions, perfectly illegal

his work perfectly legal, three hundred
thousand registered, his belt empty

of a weapon, no billy club or gun —
Yannis turns to me, says in Greek-English,

I have just one question, why do police
in America shoot their own citizens,

on the street, in the middle of the day,

at night? Fred Hampton's spirit explains,
Michael Brown testifies, I stutter.

Migrant Declaration

Regarding the EU — Turkey statement, 18 March 2016

Today migrants take collective extraordinary measure to end the human suffering. Arriving in the Greek islands

Asylum Procedures Directive, in cooperation with UNHCR migrants not applying for asylum or whose application has been found unfounded or inadmissible in accordance with the said directive will be returned to Turkey. Turkey and Greece, assisted by EU institutions and agencies, will take the necessary steps and agree any necessary bilateral arrangements, including the presence of Turkish officials on Greek islands and Greek officials in Turkey as from 20 March 2016, to ensure liaison and thereby facilitate the smooth functioning of these arrangements. The costs of the return operations of irregular migrants will be covered by the EU.

2) For every Syrian being returned to Turkey from Greek islands, another Syrian will be resettled from Turkey to the EU take into account the UN vulnerability Criteria. A mechanism will be established, with the assistance of the Commission, EU agencies and other Member States, as well as the UNHCR, to ensure that this principle will be implemented as from the same day the returns start. Priority will be given to migrants who have not previously entered or tried to enter the EU irregularly. On the EU side, resettlement under this mechanism will take place, in the first instance, by honour commitments taken by Member States in the conclusions of Representatives of the Governments of Member States meeting within the Council on 20 July 2015, of which 18.000 places for resettlement remain. Any further need for resettlement will be carried out through a similar voluntary arrangement up to a limit of an additional 54.000 persons. The Members of the European Council welcome the Commission's intention to propose an amendment to the relocation decision of 22 September 2015 to allow for any resettlement commitment undertaken in the framework of this arrangement to be offset from non-allocated places under the decision. Should these arrangements not meet the objective of ending the irregular migration and the number of returns come close to the numbers provided for above, this mechanism will be reviewed. Should the number of returns exceed the numbers provided for above, this mechanism will be discontinued.

3) Turkey will take any necessary measures to prevent new sea or land routes for illegal migration opening from Turkey to the EU, and will cooperate with neighbouring states as well as the EU to this effect.

4) Once irregular crossings. between Turkey and the EU are ending or at least have been substantially and sustainably reduced, a Voluntary Humanitarian Admission schemes will be activated. EU Member States will contribute on a voluntary basis to this scheme.

5) The fulfilment of the visa liberalisation roadmap will be accelerated vis-à-vis all participating Member States with a view to lifting the visa requirements for Turkish citizens at the latest by the end of June 2016, provided that all benchmarks have been met. To this end Turkey will take the necessary steps to fulfil the remaining requirements to allow the Commission to make, following the required assessment of compliance with the benchmarks, an appropriate proposal by the end of April on the basis of which the European Parliament and the Council can make a final decision.

6) The EU, in close cooperation with Turkey, will further speed up the disbursement of the initially allocated 3 billion euros under the Facility for Refugees in Turkey and ensure funding of further projects for persons under temporary protection identified with swift input from Turkey before the end of March. A first list of concrete projects for refugees, notably in the field of health, education, infrastructure, food and other living costs, that can be swiftly financed from the Facility, will be jointly identified within a week. Once these resources are about to be used to the full, and provided the above commitments are met, the EU will mobilise additional funding for the Facility of an additional 3 billion euro up to the end of 2018.

7) The EU and Turkey welcomed the ongoing work on the upgrading of the Customs Union.

8) The EU and Turkey reconfirmed their commitment to re-energise the accession process as set out in their joint statement of 29 November 2015. They welcomed the opening of Chapter 17 on 14 December 2015 and decided, as a next step, to open Chapter 33 during the Netherlands presidency. They welcome that the Commission will put forward a proposal to this effect in April. Preparatory work for the opening of other Chapters will continue at an accelerated pace without prejudice to Member States' positions in accordance with the existing rules.

9) The EU and its Member States will work with Turkey in any joint endeavour to improve humanitarian conditions inside Syria, in particular in certain areas near the Turkish border which would allow for the local population and refugees to live in areas which will be more safely. All these elements will be taken forward in parallel and monitored jointly on a monthly basis. The EU and Turkey decided to meet again, as necessary in accordance with the joint statement of 29 November 2015.

Part Four

Even the dead speak, "the past is infinite."

— Toni Morrison
The Source of Self-Regard

We Leave Magnolias in a Fountain

1

I write to Huda

who I met on the shore four years ago on a crowded
July day, and ask her advice for people now waiting
in Kara Tepe, since I live in a U.S. houseboat, floating in

> some reality far from a container stuck on a hillside in Mitilini,
> too hot for summer, too cold for winter, designed to entice
> madness, at the least, a yearning, sometimes hatred for what people
> can / not do for each other.

The two haiku she sends:

> Advice for people
> in the camps is a question
> I carry now.
>
> How could I hate Greece
> so much now, after loving
> her in Syria?

A UNHCR report: the average person needs 2,000 calories
per day to survive. So officials distribute 1,900.

Just enough less to keep you on edge?

Who do you borrow calories from? The baby? The elder?
The full-breasted woman?

2

I write Bashir

ask him what he remembers from the sea. He writes back, no matter
who you are, what country you came from, if smugglers kept you
in a truck for weeks, if you dodged fire in Kabul, if you carried your
elder aunt . . . no matter what, the sea was the worst, our arrival, the gift:

    disaster the sea / glorious, the shore

    the chop . . . the pitch . . . the storm / the hands . . . the rope . . . the sand

    my daughter curls inside my vest / she runs with pipits by the rocks

    gasoline soaks our tired clothes / wildflowers preach to a quiet beach

    sarin gas on frightened skin / we leave magnolias in a fountain.

3

I write a supervisor

about translator rates so we can teach Darwish and Jordan in the poetry class.
It is customary, he says, to pay five euros per hour. The teachers only get ten.
If you pay more, you send a confusing message.

> The translator arrives, a professor in Afghanistan, his perfectly clipped
> beard, his British English, he who speaks and writes in Pashto,
> Urdu, Persian, and Hindi.

> When my eyes say help, after people start to fidget, after the whiteboard
> marker gives up, after we run out of pencils, he begins to recite Nye
> in Dari so those who can't read might float a poem above their chairs.

4

after class, my energy evaporated, I ask, *where will you rest?*

> *Back at my container, safer than the forest*
> *where we cowered when they fired on us*
> *and better than forty-five days in an Iranian jail.*

He shows a photo of his wife, her gardenia petal nails
scrubbing his Oxford shirt.

Their container is white tin on the outside, white tin
on the inside, no insulation. No electricity. No Internet.
No rugs. No windows. No sky.

> *We're lucky. We are here.*

5

the view from Mitilini

a holiday for the wealthy.
I take the bus back to Eftalou.
Gaze out a window
scratched by granite and salt.

Each Day Lessons in Greek

Ignatio says, first we name the cats — mother
and three kittens — Leeza, Chrissa, Beba and Lola.
I practice *the soil on the mountain is not good
for farming. The earth in the garden is rich*. Today,
we focus on ah-crow-care-eh-mo, monuments
on rooftop corners. Mary says they're for beauty.
Sculptures of women with buxom breasts.

Ignatio says even churches have gargoyles.
In the old days women didn't wear blouses.
Panselinos, the hotel down the road, means full
moon, which is tonight. Each day lessons in Greek,
a blue book full now. We start with *the garden
is beautiful*. And *today is hot*. Then, *the cats play*.
And, *this is honeysuckle*. Then, *Monday is your first
yoga class and you'll ride your bike*. And *Mary picks
strawberries for her mother*. And *Ignatio was born in
Kalloni*. And, *today the waves are wild*. And *Becky
writes poems about people moving across this island*.

Ignatio laughs when I can't say the letter x, insists
on proper pronunciation, waits as I sound out
sentences. Slaps the air when I play with words.
Service in English relates to a car or a gathering
at a church. Den xero (I don't know)
is my favorite expression. Ignatio claims, *If Becky
speaks Greek now, she will write Greek next year*.
On the morning seven people drown in dinghies
off the Mitilini coast, he teaches me, *I am very sorry
for this*. We practice *Yiayia keeps company with the sea
and remembers everything*. The word for happy —
charoumena. And *this is the word for artichoke*.

Perhaps someday I'll be able to ask Ignatio in Greek
about his family. Who died in the Turkish genocide.
The survivors fled across the Aegean to Kalloni where
he drives every Sunday to sing tenor at his church.
One day I'll ask him about the shoes. How
he discovered me serving scrambled eggs and
croissants to thirteen people from Syria and Iraq
in my Sun House room. We planned to eat quickly
then walk to Molyvos before dawn, except I forgot
about thirteen pairs of shoes outside my door. And
that Ignatio wakes before the cats. My eyes traced the
floor when he came in, afraid I'd offended my host.

Ten minutes later, Ignatio left, returned with milk
for the children. As we left he motioned with his hands
(no words in English) *avoid the police, send the family*
to the right, you go left so no one sees you together.
He counts with his fingers, *my family, fourteen died.*

That winter Ignatio waded into the Eftalou sea
in front of the Sun House, cradling a three-year-old boy.
Later, Ignatio discovered a journalist had snapped
his photo, put it on the cover of an international
magazine. Mary had the photo framed. It's propped
between the fireplace and the ironing board.

Ekphrastic

for Emmanuel

The photo would be of you and me
standing under wisteria, sea

like a drape in the background, cats sacked
out in the shade, our arms looped

after you whispered your testimonial
and I typed into an overheated laptop.

Only there could be no snapshot,
your red soccer shirt and my linen

shorts made for Greece in June,
the two of us formal and shy.

No hug for the child, your adult
face closed by orders to spy

on families, their intimate rhythms,
where they washed and prayed, when

their children tumbled home from
school, the St. Finbarr Church on

a suicide bomber's list, barbed
wire wrapped around Boko

Haram's prey, the child vanished
in explosions you escaped.

How Ganesha Works

May I ask for a love letter to the painter who tied
her six children to her belly with a jump rope

before stepping inside the raft, saying they
would all reach shore or go down together?

So many poems veer toward sadness, doves
seeking a water fountain gone dry.

But then, four sons, and their Syrian mother,
who dodged smugglers, swam their dinghy to

shore, announce yes, we escaped without
my husband, after he took me in snatches.

The elephant god traces a path.

She Asks Jizo Bosatsu

What to do with her body now the dinghies
have stopped their furious pace? For three
seasons she'd biked the seacoast road,
chased rafts, walked with families up
Petra Highway. Now rafts that slip past
the military's neon eyes are banished like
uninvited relatives at a wedding. She
stares at Turkey's coast, wonders about
mothers who sell shoes in Istanbul,
lament Syria, count unschooled seasons.

She buries stones in sand to zigzag a path,
stacks rocks into faces and stout bodies,
balanced to weather wind, like Jizo statues
in Japan, Moai carved stones on Rapa Nui.

These cairns, opal and obsidian, named
after people she misses, shaped like the arch
at Hisham's Palace and Parthenon columns.
During storms stones topple like unpracticed
gymnasts, their falls redesign the coastline.

Might those still standing chat with fishermen,
howl at the sea, send love letters to the Bent
Pyramid, grieve for the Great Mosque of Aleppo?

On her last evening, anise adorns the road,
this island's sunflower. The new moon traces
its solstice sky. She glances into a rowboat
marooned on a beach, #safepassagenow
scrawled on its side, a pair of infant sandals
cradled inside. Her mind tumbles like rocks

that refuse to stack. Do shoes stay on a girl's
feet as she goes down, or wiggle free?

What cairn for such a thing?

At the Sea, Shazia Whispers

from across this island I traipse
to Eftalou like a homing pigeon drawn
to a grave. The sea wakes

my fear but look at my Alia, she's a swan
in the waves, will float until she learns
to butterfly, her spirit tries on

anything new, while I yearn
for before when we pleated rice and peas,
we loved in a valley with sweet ferns,

eucalyptus and mango fields, we
lived with electric gates and bodyguards
until bullets traveled through my beloved. Carefree.

Alia and I escaped through a night's scar,
traveled far, now I think in allegory
of the Trojan and a fanciful horse, filled with stars.

As for this beach, what then of tiny boxes, tiny
graves? What then of bones that anchors abut?
These questions like jiggers that leave faint lines.

The Aegean venetian blinds I cannot draw shut.

Once Her Children Are Asleep,
Fatma Picks Up Her Paintbrush

A people without
a homeland is like dates
on a forgotten tree
sweetness left to wither
falling on white phosphorus ground.

Gathering, Incantation

Years later we will be drawn to Seaweed Beach
where generations landed or slipped under,
the boy who played behind the weeping beech
now a father with a daughter who wonders.

Where generations landed or slipped under,
there's a boy who told stories of imaginary creatures
now a father with a daughter who wonders
about Turkey and Greece, her squint a permanent feature.

The boy who told stories of imaginary creatures
tells tales of a woman who could see the future
about Turkey and Greece, her squint a permanent feature,
who sees the sea as a ribbon, a maritime suture.

There are stories of a woman who could see the future,
the spirits of children who clap ancient rhythms;
sees the sea as a ribbon, a maritime suture,
the tides a body with new algorithms.

The spirits of children who clap ancient rhythms
announce a party for elders and recent arrivals.
The tides embody new algorithms
that include the dead and those who insist on survival.

If you announce a party for elders and recent arrivals
include the boy who played behind the weeping beech.
Honor the dead and those who insist on survival
so years later, we will be drawn to Seaweed Beach.

What the Sky Watches

Sunrise on my face, a Minoan pot shape shifts into a mosque.
Poseidon winds chase whitecaps coming up for air, the sea bottom laughs.
Up cobblestone steps, rosaries become a man's talisman, each quiet flick.
Women without wings paste eagle feathers to their arms, scoop up children.
Cats meditate in summer, hide in winter rain, love and fight like humans.
Swallows embroider nests they return to each year; babies know they're home.
Heavy summer air, let strife be lonely, sidewalks sing to the streets.
I cry for the world fragile as a starfish left alone by the tide.
Without my ozone I'd be as helpless as a baby left alone.
If water covers the islands sea urchins will host bigger conventions.
The moon makes stars shy with their beauty; the sun misses the etude.
Zeus says, *Atlas, hold heaven on your shoulders, a new weathered map.*
Tonight, a steady stream of people walk across the setting sun.
We are all connected to the center of the earth, each precious one.

Wrapped in Clouds

Since leaving
          seeing babies in strollers
is the hardest.
          They cry and laugh
as if they were
          wrapped in clouds.
I remember ones
          whose limbs twitched
quiet as a breeze
          on a pond. My
body is a statue
          filled with tears. I wake
not knowing
          if I'm on a raft
or waiting
          for one.
Do I pray
          people come, escaping
another despot
          or do I pray
they stay, this
          island trembling
without tourists?
          Do I pray they
come, after years
          in detention —
or do I pray they
          stay, leaky tents
and no food?

Do I pray they come

that water will

carry or do I pray they

stay, waves

will menace?

Do I pray?

In the Arc of Lost Time Blue Holes Gather

the consciousness of those who made it

the strait between Turkey and Lesvos

the rafts, whale's teeth, the water

I return like I never left

Their hours of terror last longer

Inside the whale, time absorbs a new

the clock slows down and speeds up

from the world, like the Battle

the beating of a child, that

Rumi's couplets, Weiwei's human flow.

honor too big a word for poets to earn

we are caught inside, we

new, so much lost when

words too, more than we can live with —

to the sea, over and over, not done.

all the sea cannot bear

and did not

the whale's mouth

and its power to decide.

asking, were you there?

than a lifetime.

dimension, birth and death collide

demands we find words vanished

of Dunkirk, the Sand Creek massacre

we weave memory into quilts

Art cannot bring back the dead

more like humble moments

try to shrink horror into something

people leave their homelands, to lose

like a two-tailed swallow, returning

Return
after Du Fu

Wake to / blank wall / sea floods
night vision / raft dizzy / dot sinks

insistent calls / lighthouse sounds / birds seek
fish eat / light candle / starless land

travel / take me / faint song
ancient channel / to god reach / choppy water

mind quiets / Aegean return / tide rests
teal light / weathered / before dawn

morning / black tea / turns to you

Lesvos

after Zeyn Joukhadar

When I was born
a glacier carved my
shape like a winter tulip, so
I could still see Anatolia, my eight sisters each
a tortoise step for the gods. I am my mother's daughter, here
before volcanoes let loose. Lava domes are now castles to the sky.
Sea of my dreams, with your fierce moods and sequined days, I am the
poet's land, the home of Arion's meter and Terpander's musical scale. There
was a time when the people rotated crops like verses in holiday hymns. There was
a time when men were pretty and women were strong. There was a time before the
Byzantines and Ottomans.   When gargoyles cavorted with cats who mated and then
slept. Sea of my dreams, I long for boats that bring tilapia and cod.   For beaches that
sing rain, recycle wind with long breath.   When the moonflower shines, the moment
will awaken your spine.   As long as you come   you are welcome.
Flamingos will be waiting   and early mist, night   shades so black
they shimmer. Sea of my   dreams welcome all   who come to my shores.
As olive trees reach   from China to   Australia, so do my arms.
This island is too big.   This island is   too small.
There   is always   room.

96

Endnotes to the Poems

p. 20: "A Litany Travels" references Audre Lorde's "Litany for Survival," one of the poems Sayed Naweed Balkhi translated into Pashto and Dari for the poetry classes (from *The Collected Poems of Audre Lorde*, Norton, 1997). The Somali teen's allusion to a "poem about memories and backpacks" references Zeina Azzam, "Leaving My Childhood Home" in *Making Mirrors: Righting / Writing by and for Refugees*, edited by Jehan Bseiso and Becky Thompson (Interlink, 2019).

p. 22: "Layla Asks, *Why Are We Here If We Didn't Do Anything Wrong*" references the lines *We who believe in freedom cannot rest* from Sweet Honey in the Rock's "Ella's Song." *YouTube*, https://www.youtube.com/watch?v=1tG1dNJh2rw.

p. 30: "Jamil Says, *We Wait in Line*" is a Golden Shovel in honor of "We Real Cool" by Gwendolyn Brooks and Joy Harjo's "An American Sunrise." *Clouds looking for a way out, gotta play no matter the sway of forces* is from "The Soul Travelers — A Way Out / Gale Sayers (Live Acoustic)." *YouTube*, https://www.youtube.com/watch?v=cAeXYp3kCok.

p. 31: "Ghazal: Asylum for the Youngest Brother" celebrates the occasion of Jalal Joinda's brother gaining asylum in Greece after a prolonged threat of deportation. *See* Joinda, Jalal. "Jalal Joinda a song refugees song." *YouTube*, https://www.youtube.com/watch?v=YANREeSa5rw.

p. 34: "Solidarity, (For)ever: "feminist as tourist," "feminist as explorer," and "feminist in solidarity" comes from Chandra Mohanty, "'Under Western Eyes' Revisited: Feminist Solidarity through Anticapitalist Struggles," *Signs: Journal of Women in Culture and Society* 2002, vol. 28, no. 2, 499-535.

p. 43: "*We Have Taken the One in the Sky as Our Witness*" — Italicized lines from "Syrian Poet and Actor Fadwa Souleiman, 45." *Arablit Quarterly*, 17 Aug. 2017, https://arablit.org/2017/08/17/fadwa-souleiman. The title is from "From Genesis" in *Making Mirrors: Righting/Writing by and for Refugees*, edited by Jehan Bseiso and Becky Thompson (Interlink, 2019).

p. 44: "Hold onto Time" references the work of Yara Badr, Mazen Darwish, and their colleagues at the Syrian Center for Media and Freedom of Expression. *See* Yara Badr and Mazen Darwish, "Lifetimes Stolen" and "Letter for the Future" in *Syria Speaks: Art and Culture from the Frontline*, edited by Malu Halasa, Zaher Omareen and Nawara Mahfoud (Saqi, 2014), 192-204.

p. 45: "Carola Rackete Takes the Microphone" references the German ship captain who is among the maritime rescue workers whose humanitarian work has been criminalized since 2016.

p. 46: "*Winnipeg*" — The *Winnipeg* was a steamer commissioned by Pablo Neruda to carry 2,200 people from danger in Europe to Chile in 1939. About the ship Neruda wrote, "From the beginning I liked the word Winnipeg. Words either have wings or they don't. The word Winnipeg is winged." See Desimone, Arturo. "Valparaíso-bound: Neruda's ark." *OpenDemocracy*, https://www.opendemocracy.net/arturo-desimone/valpara-so-bound-neruda-s-ark.

p. 52: "*Loving in Doorways*" — This poem borrows words from "A Litany of Survival": *in our children's mouths / so their dreams will not reflect / the death of ours* and *coming and going / in the hours between dawns* in *The Collected Poems of Audre Lorde* (Norton, 1997).

p. 54: "Report from Sona" is dedicated to an eight-year-old I met from Guinea-Bissau.

p. 60: "In Moria We Have Cats" is dedicated to the fourteen-year-old who wrote the landay in a poetry workshop, *Work for yourself not others / Tomorrow no one will be friends with you.*

p. 61: "Celan Travels" — The last line references *you teach you teach your hand to sleep*, from Tarfia Faizullah, "Reading Celan at the Liberation War Museum." *Seam* (Crab Orchard Review, Southern Illinois University Press, 2014).

p. 66: "How Shall We Divide This Bounty" — Nadia Ghulam is an award-winning writer and a magical storyteller, a talent I witnessed when we co-led talking circles for women and their children in a storeroom at the Hope Project in Mitilini.

p. 70: "A Father Asks" — Before the EU closed its borders in 2016, the most common route that people traveled (by bus, train, or foot) was from Greece to Macedonia, to Serbia, to Croatia, to Austria, to Germany. After the borders closed, many families in Mitilini or Athens were taken to abandoned hotels in remote areas of Greece where they were vulnerable to backlash by anti-immigrant groups. Often, their only choice was to escape, typically at night, in hopes of making it to more northern EU countries.

p. 72: "Migrant Declaration" references the 2016 EU - Turkey Statement negotiated by several countries that resulted in Turkey receiving incentives to stop passage of people from Turkey to Greece. Key Balkan states closed access to people in transit as did Austria, Germany, France, Norway, the UK and other countries. Tens of thousands of people continue to risk passage from Turkey to Greece each year amidst pushbacks (rafts in the Aegean dragged back to Turkey) and deportation of refugees by sea by Greek officials. A similar restriction between Libya and Italy was codified in 2017, further jeopardizing safe passage on that route.

p. 96: "Lesvos" references the sacred maps in Zeyn Joukhadar's beautiful novel *The Map of Salt and Stars* (Touchstone, 2018).

Words in Arabic, Dari, Farsi, Greek, Susu, and Urdu

Forms in square brackets are additional transcriptions. In the text, we chose not to italicize words to designate a shift in language, allowing them to coexist on an equal plane.

aietidhar (Arabic): I'm sorry (literally, apology).

Bood nabood (Dari): Once upon a time (literally, there was, there was not).

charoumena (Greek): cheerful, happy.

den xero (Greek): I don't know.

dooset daram (Farsi): I love you.

habibti (Arabic): My love.

kalimera (Greek): Good morning!

khoda hafez (Farsi): Goodbye! (literally, God be your guardian!).

khosh amadid (Farsi): Welcome! (literally, Well you came!).

milh (Arabic): salt.

mushaira (Urdu): traditional poetry symposium.

ngoni (Susu): traditional guitar from Mali.

panselinos (Greek): full moon.

Salaam Alaikum (Arabic): Peace be with you.

salat (Arabic): daily prayer.

souq (Arabic): street market.

tabouleh (Arabic): Levantine salad of bulgur wheat, tomatoes, parsley, olive oil, lemon juice, and salt.

ti kaneis (Greek): How are you? (literally, What are you doing?).

vitrina (Greek): curtain, e.g. in shop window.

xenos (Greek): stranger, foreigner, guest.

yiayia [Giagia] (Greek): grandmother.

zouhourat [zhourat] (Arabic): herbal tea made with hibiscus flowers.

Map of Lesvos, Greece

Showing cities, roads, and refugee camps mentioned in the text.

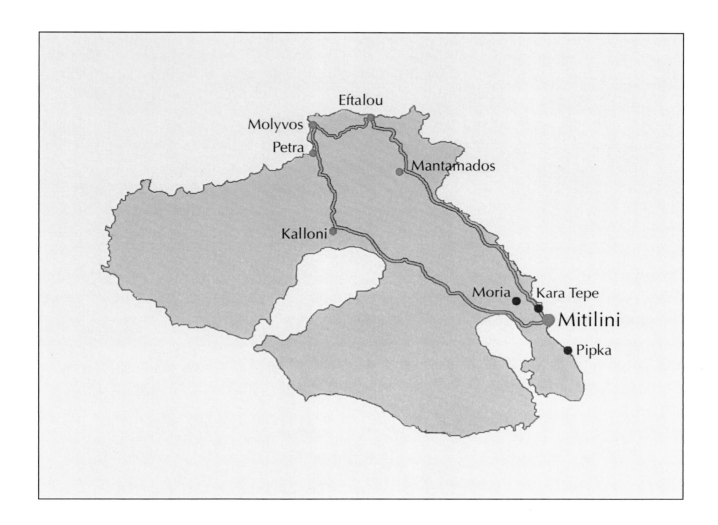

Place Names

Forms in square brackets are additional transcriptions.

Aleppo: ancient, cosmopolitan city in northwestern Syria, the largest city in Syria until the mass exodus during the civil war.

Bent Pyramid: the Southern Shining Pyramid in Egypt just south of Cairo, built with limestone in 2600 BCE; its design reflects a transition from step-sided (staircase to the stars) architecture to smooth (from the earth, the source of all life) architecture.

Bashira House / Bashira Centre: site of a feminist NGO in Lesvos providing assistance to asylum-seeking women and children; home of privacy, soft couches, and tea.

Dadaab: in eastern Kenya, the world's largest refugee city/center in the world (275,000 people), first established in 1991 during the civil war in Somalia. As described by an activist born there, "Dadaab is a place where many people are born and die, where people make life with sticks and stones."

Damascus: the oldest capital in the world; a major cultural center in Syria and surrounding countries; home of several universities and the largest Palestinian community in Syria; one of the cities most damaged during the Syrian war.

Eftalou: tiny village in northern Lesvos, home of Seaweed Beach, just across from the Turkish coast; known for its hot springs, wildflowers, and breath-giving views.

Exarchia Square [**Exarcheia Square**]: large square in Athens with anarchist, intellectual, artistic roots; a gathering location for many asylum seekers.

Great Mosque of Aleppo (**Jāmiʼ Ḥalab al-Kabīr***)*: built in the eighth century CE in what is now a World Heritage site near the entrance to Al-Madina Souq in Aleppo; partially destroyed in the Syrian war.

Gulf of Adramiti [**Gulf of Adramyti**, **Gulf of Adramyttium**, **Edremit Gulf**]: Aegean Sea gulf northeast of Lesvos near Edremit, Turkey.

Hisham's Palace: an early Islamic, eighth-century palace ruin close to Jericho on the West Bank, Palestine.

Hope Project: art center, clothing and food distribution center on the outskirts of Mitilini, Greece; begun by Philippa and Eric Kempson and staffed by asylum seekers and their advocates.

Hotel Daedalip: a pseudonym for one of the rural hotels in Greece that allowed asylum seekers to stay temporarily despite backlash from neighbors. *Daedalip* is derived from Daedalus in Greek mythology, an inventor, craftsman and father of Icarus, who flew too close to the sun and drowned in the Mediterranean.

Idlib: city in northwestern Syria; home of cherries, white helmets, and ancient tells (small hills holding sediment from earlier generations).

Izmir: Mediterranean city in western Turkey, known in classical times as Smyrna; burnt to the ground during the genocide of Armenians and Greeks in the early 1920s (part of what is euphemistically called the "Population Exchange" between Turkey and Greece).

Jalalabad: a sunny city in northeastern Afghanistan; the home of Nangarhar University, the second largest in the country, with a rich tradition of Afghan poetry; known for its mangoes, oil, and rice.

Kabul: the capital of Afghanistan; a city of epics and pride.

Kalloni: town in west-central Lesvos, halfway between Molyvos and Mitilini, the third town on the (walking) route across the island. Kalloni is known for its flamingos, sardines and two historic monasteries, Saint Ignatios and Myrsiniotissa.

Kara Tepe: overcrowded refugee camp for families just north of Mitilini run by the Municipality of Mitilini and the UNHCR; has served as temporary residence (tents and containers) for tens of thousands of people since 2015; considered a step up in terms of safety and health from Moria.

Khora: collectively run community center in Athens that offers language and poetry classes, home-cooked meals, and legal support for people affected by the European border regime.

Latakia Harbor: the main seaport of Syria, in the city of Latakia, on the Mediterranean Sea.

Lesvos [Lesbos]: among the easternmost of the Greek islands, twelve kilometers from the Turkish coast; historic crossroads for birds, languages, and people seeking safety.

Life Jacket Graveyard: a locally named expanse on a hill overlooking the sea in Eftalou, Lesvos, where sanitation workers brought tens of thousands of life jackets from Lesvos shores.

Mantamados: small town in northeastern Lesvos.

Mitilini [Mytilini]: the capital of Lesvos; the primary entry point for asylum seekers looking for passage to Athens; the location of Moria, Kara Tepe, and Pipka; an increasingly multiethnic city since 2015.

Molyvos: village built around a Byzantine castle in northern Lesvos; the Molyvos Harbor is where asylum seekers registered before walking to Mitilini.

Mythimna Road: the road leading out of Molyvos to Petra, laced with monastery fountains, farmland, olive trees, and dramatic inclines.

Moria: a district in Mitilini and the former site of the Moria Refugee Camp, temporary residence for people from multiple Middle Eastern and African countries. Originally intended for 3,000 people (in 2015), its residents often included more than 15,000 people staying in tents and makeshift structures. Moria was destroyed by fire in October 2020. Maryam Janikhushk, former Moria organizer, described Moria's end: "The last leaves of the trees fell and winter came and the trees fell asleep."

Mosaik Centre: cultural center on a cobble street in Mitilini that offers Greek, English, Farsi and Arabic classes, writing and poetry workshops, cinema nights, and social support for asylum seekers.

Petra: small coastal town in northern Lesvos, six kilometers south of Molyvos, on the route from Eftalou to Mitilini for asylum seekers.

Pipka Camp: also known as Lesvos Solidarity, was a children's holiday camp that became the temporary residence for the most vulnerable asylum seekers; known as a relatively safe space that provided quiet, warm food, and medical and psychological support.

Rapa Nui [**Easter Island**]: A Polynesian island in the southeastern Pacific Ocean off the coast of Chile renowned for its nine hundred moai, majestic hand-carved stone statues that resemble human figures resting on stone pedestals.

Qamishli: multilingual, multiethnic city in northeastern Syria, on the Turkish border.

Seaweed Beach: soft-landing beach covered with dried seaweed between Minoli's Taverna and the Sun House in Eftalou; one of the safer spots along the Lesvos coast for rafts coming to shore.

Thessaloniki: northern Greek city, the second largest in Greece; home to universities, art, poetry, and Elpida Home, a nonprofit, safe residence for vulnerable families.

Victoria Square: well-known square in Athens and meeting place for newcomers; home of the sculpture *Theseus Saving Hippodamia*.

Names of People

Arion (seventh century BCE): legendary Greek poet and inventor of the ancient Greek hymn form known as the dithyramb; a native of Lesvos.

Awesome Qasim: Afghan musician who raps in Pashto, Persian, and English. Recordings are available on *YouTube*.

Badr, Yara (b. 1985): Syrian journalist and human rights activist, founder (with her husband Mazen Darwish) of the Syrian Center for Media and Freedom of Expression in Damascus (2004). She now lives in exile in Berlin.

Balkhi, Sayed Naweed: literature professor in Afghanistan who worked as a translator/co-teacher at the Mosaik Centre in Mitilini.

Brown, Michael (1996-2014): eighteen-year-old Black man fatally murdered by Ferguson, Missouri police; his murder sparked major uprisings against police brutality.

Celan, Paul (1920-1970): Romanian born German-language poet whose works wrestle with the survival of language and the human spirit in the face of cruelty and disaster.

Darwish, Mahmoud (1941-2008): preeminent lyric, epic and elegiac Palestinian poet whose writing offers an exquisite witness of diaspora and belonging.

Diabaté, Sona (b. 1959): a griot Guinean musician who founded the group *Les Amazones de Guinée*. Recordings are available on *YouTube*.

Dido: legendary queen and founder of Carthage, currently in Tunisia; lover of Aeneas in Virgil's *Aeneid*.

Du Fu (712-770): Tang-Dynasty Chinese poet. Du Fu and his friend Li Bai are considered the two greatest Chinese poets.

Erdogan, Recep Tayyip (b. 1954): president of Turkey since 2014.

Farmer, Angela (b. 1939): revered elder yogini who lives and teaches in Eftalou, Greece with her partner, the artist Victor van Kooten.

Frank, Anne [*Annelies Marie Frank*] (1929-1945): Dutch author of *Het Achterhuis* [*The Diary of a Young Girl*], published posthumously in 1947; killed in the Holocaust.

Ghulam, Nadia (b. 1985): Barcelona-based Afghan author of *The Secret of My Turban*. The book presents her ten years passing as her deceased brother under Taliban rule so she could study and work to support her family.

Guébo, Josué (b. 1972): Ivorian poet, playwright, and essayist.

Hafiz [Khwāje Shams-od-Dīn Mohammad Hāfez-e Shīrāzī] (1315-1390): major Persian Sufi poet and mystic; he primarily wrote in ghazals.

Hampton, Fred (1948-1969): charismatic young Black Panther Party leader and founder of the Rainbow Coalition; assassinated in his bed by the Chicago police.

Joinda family: an Afghan family living in exile in Greece and India. Several family members are active in filmmaking, acting, and music. Songs by Jalal Joinda are available on *YouTube*.

Jordan, June (1936-2002): luminary Black poet, essayist, professor, activist and founder of Poetry for the People.

Joukhadar, Zeyn: Syrian-American writer; author of *The Map of Salt and Stars*; recipient of the 2021 Lambda Literary Award for his book *The Thirty Names of Night*.

Lorde, Audre (1934-1992): Black lesbian feminist poet and writer in the U.S. known for her passionate and prophetic writing.

Kazantzoglou, Ignatios (b. 1934): owner with his wife, Maria Kontou Nikolaos, of the Sun House on the Aegean coast in Eftalou, Greece.

Kurdi, Alan [Alan Shenu] (b. 2012): a Kurdish Syrian three-year-old who drowned in 2015 while his family attempted to reach Greece by raft.

Morrison, Toni (1931-2019): Nobel laureate African-American writer, author of eleven novels including *Beloved* (1987).

Nye, Naomi Shihab (b. 1952): Palestinian-American poet, novelist and the Young People's Poet Laureate (2019-2021).

Rackete, Carola (b. 1988): German ship captain active with the rescue organization Sea-Watch, arrested in 2019 for docking a rescue ship in the port of Lampedusa, Italy.

Rumi [Jalāl ad-Dīn Mohammad Balkhi] (1207-1273): Persian poet and a voice of Sufism, born in what is now Afghanistan.

Sappho (c. 630-c. 570 BCE): Greek lyric poet and native of Lesvos; regarded in her own day and still, as a major poet, even though few of her works survive.

Shakur, Tupac (1971-1996): visionary U.S. rapper and actor, an inspiration globally.

Soul Travelers, The (2012-present): rap-soul-jazz group from Amsterdam by way of Namibia; songs include "What I Am / Sofar Amsterdam" with the emblematic lyric, *in the eyes of my eyes we all gods, all good, all hoods, ready to rise.*

Sweet Honey in the Rock (1973-present): visionary a cappella African-American performance ensemble founded by Dr. Bernice Johnson Reagon; quintessential sound track for multiracial feminism.

Taxiarchis (St. Michael Taxiarchis): patron saint of Lesvos. An icon in his honor is found in the Byzantine monastery in Mantamados.

Terpander (seventh century BCE): developer of the Greek musical modes; a native of Lesvos.

Wallace, George (1919-1998): four-term governor of Alabama (1970-1982); white supremacist who ran for president of the U.S. as a Democrat three times.

Weiwei, Ai (b. 1957): Chinese artist and activist whose prolific works include the film *Human Flow* and the exhibit *Law of the Journey*.

Wiesel, Elie (1928-2016): Romanian-born American writer, Holocaust survivor, and Nobel laureate. Author of *Night* (1960) and other major works.

Publication Acknowledgements

*Grateful acknowledgement is made to the following journals,
where these poems originally appeared.*

An earlier version of "Teaching Poetry at Khora" was published in "'I tied my children to my body': The continuing courage of refugees in Greece," *Anchor Magazine: Where spirituality and social justice meet*, 8, fall/winter (2017), 78-80.

An earlier version of "Ahmad Talks to His 13-Year-Old Brother" published in *CURA*, Issue 20, (2019). Thank you, Jennifer Tseng.

"Solidarity (For)ever," and "A Litany Travels" in *Feminist Formations*. Fatima El-Tayeb and Maria Stehle, eds. Spring, Vol. 34, no. 1 (2022).

An earlier version of "Cartography in Lesvos" was published in *Feminist Studies,* Vol. 46, no. 2 (2020). Thank you to Alexis Pauline Gumbs and Ashwini Tambe.

"Squatters' Rights" appeared in *Making Mirrors: Righting/Writing by and for Refugees*, edited by Jehan Bseiso and Becky Thompson (Interlink, 2019).

"Haiku Questions" in *Pensive: A Global Journal of Spirituality and the Arts* (2021).

"Hold onto Time" appeared in *Sonora Review,* special issue on gender-based violence (2021). https://sonorareview.com/extinction/.

"Wrapped in Clouds," "What the Sky Watches," "In the Arc of Lost Time Blue Holes Gather," "The Accompanied Minor Wonders" in *Soul Forte: An Online Journal of Spiritual Writing*, Issue 1 (2021).

"Jamil Says, *We Wait in Line*" in *Stonecoast Review*, Issue 14 (2021).

"A Greek Coast Guard Officer Asks" in *Visions International: The World Journal of Illustrated Poetry*, Issue 104 (2021).

About the Author

Photo by Edgar Peraza

Becky Thompson, MFA, Ph.D., is a poet, human rights activist, yogi, and professor. She is the author of several books, most recently *Teaching with Tenderness* and *Survivors on the Yoga Mat*. She has co-edited two poetry anthologies, including *Making Mirrors: Righting/Writing by and for Refugees* (with Jehan Bseiso). Her honors include the Gustavus Myers Award for Outstanding Books on Human Rights and fellowships from the Rockefeller Foundation, the National Endowment for the Humanities, and the American Association of University Women. She has held appointments at China Women's University, Princeton University, Duke University, and the University of Colorado, and currently teaches at Simmons University. Since 2015 Becky has been traveling to Greece, meeting rafts, working with asylum seekers, and teaching poetry workshops. For more see beckythompsonyoga.com.

This book was printed on 80-pound white Lynx opaque ultra-smooth paper at Bookmobile in Minneapolis, MN. The text is set in Minion Pro with display in Optima.